God Is Bigger Than Your FBI

by

Tracy L. Baldwin

Former FBI Special Agent

www.TracyBaldwin.com

God Is Bigger Than Your FBI

ISBN: 978-0-6151-8766-2

Library of Congress Control Number: 2008900716

Printed in the United States of America

The Federal Bureau of Investigation (FBI) has no objection to
this publication. The views expressed do not necessarily
represent the views of the FBI.

♋♋♋♋♋♋

- ♦ Cover photograph courtesy of RVforSaleGuide.com
- ♦ Cover graphics by Franc Reyes: FrancReyestx@gmail.com
- ♦ Headshot by DebbiePorter.com

♋♋♋♋♋♋

In Loving Memory

Of

Roy Gene Baldwin

August 1, 1936 – July 29, 2007

❧ *To My Amazing Family* ❧

My beautiful mother, Joan, who's been my lifelong beacon of light ~ my big sister, Natalie, who has walked with me through the good and bad ~ my big brother, Jeff, who has been a living example of a Godly man ~ his wife, Stacy, and children, Hudson, Stephanie & Katherine. Thanks to each of you for living your faith in God, for your love and continual support. You've given me strength to make this difficult journey.

❧ *To My Spiritual Leaders* ❧

Dr. Jimmy Jackson, Whitesburg Baptist Church, Huntsville, AL: you've helped and guided me for more than 20 years. Thank you for your strength and patience . . . and for leading me to a closer walk with the Lord through every trial. *Psalm 46*

Joel Osteen, Lakewood Church, Houston, TX: you've helped me in my darkest hours. Thank you for always reminding me that I am a child of the most high God and He has me in the palm of His hand.
Jeremiah 29:11

❧ *To My Friends & Family in the Lord* ❧

Deree, Brenda, Kathleen, Kathy, Tony, Garry, Sherry, Melanie, Susan, Tom (YOD) & Cheri, Joni & Scott, Judy & George, Ellen, Denise, Juliana, Cheryl & John & Shelly, Dawn, Wendell, Chad, Javier, Luke & Bethany, Joanna, Janet, the Lakewood Players, Craig & Sam, Rudy, Harold, Debbie, Wayne, Chip, Ashlee, Geneve, Jackie, Sarah, Adana, Linda, Lynette, Ruth, Shonna, Joe & Dell Mara, Michael and the many others who have touched and changed my life:
Thank you . . . for Everything!

❧ *and My Incredible Attorney* ❧

Charles T. Jeremiah

Contents

࿔࿔࿔࿔࿔࿔

❧ *Introduction* ❧

*For I know the plans I have for you," declares the LORD,
"plans to prosper you and not to harm you, plans to give
you hope and a future." Jeremiah 29:11 (NIV)*

❧❧❧❧❧❧

It's not easy to write about what happened during my nine years as an FBI Special Agent (SA). Besides revisiting some excruciating experiences, I've had numerous concerns. My family and friends have expressed concerns with a much more ominous tone. I've seen that powerful institution we know as the Federal Bureau of Investigation (FBI) freely participate in deceit, lies and manipulation – so just how far will they go? I continue to put my trust in the God of *TRUTH* for His protection:

> *The LORD will keep you from all harm— He will watch over your life; the LORD will watch over your coming and going both now and forevermore. Psalm 121: 7-8 (NIV)*

I was raised in a very proud, solid family with service in every branch of the military. Family values have always been important and my parents were together for over 51 years. They taught me at an early age about the value of hard work, developing a thick skin, to keep a stiff upper lip, and to do the right thing.

Not to say I didn't make blunders along the way . . . I made plenty of bad choices, almost exclusively about men in romantic relationships. However, even through the most difficult times, I've lived my life with integrity, honesty and fairness.

In my early teens my father was stationed in Kuwait. It was an adventure to say the least. As Americans we were treated like royalty and we even had a red carpet rolled out on the tarmac when our plane arrived.

My brother, sister and I attended the American School of Kuwait (ASK), paid for by the US Government. Kids in the US may learn about some other cultures, but we had living teachers in our best friends . . . from the US, Kuwait, Egypt, Norway, Sweden, etc. I was on the ASK basketball team and rather than play against other schools in Kuwait, our team was flown to challenge schools in Bahrain and

1

Dubai. We stayed with host families, many that didn't speak English. We learned to communicate through gestures – a sloppy sign language of sorts. It was my first lesson in understanding that you don't have to know what someone says with their mouth to see clearly into their heart.

We spent a lot of time at the American Embassy, guarded by Kuwaiti soldiers garnishing rifles with razor sharp bayonets. As young kids we thought all that was kinda cool and often laughed and joked with the soldiers. They kept a professional distance until we all tried to climb over the Embassy wall . . . they didn't think that was very funny. We were too young to fully understand the danger surrounding us even when we got a day off at school or dad came home early because of a bomb scare.

We had some amazing opportunities while we were in Kuwait . . . like when we met Pittsburgh Stealers football players Lynn Swann, Andy Russell and Ray Mansfield. I have no idea why they were there, and we didn't ask questions . . . we were just excited to hang out with them at the pool and play football.

Our "goals" for the big football game were two trees on either side of a grassy area by the tennis courts. I was on Andy Russell's team, my brother Jeff was on Lynn Swann's team. At one point, I got the ball and was running toward the tree goal. Lynn grabbed me around the waist for the tackle. Even then I was a determined little gal so I kept trudging forward. Lynn didn't want to hurt me so he held me around the waist as I continued to inch toward the goal. Jeff came barreling over and tackled both of us. Now Jeff has bragging rights that he tackled Lynn Swann. Talk about good sports . . . those guys were amazing. We also met several of the Globe Trotters, as well as astronauts. These were my first lessons that "big" or "famous" people were still just that . . . people. They didn't have an entourage and there were no "lights & cameras" when we ate and laughed together. Even the "high level officials" were just people. They came to the events and plays we put on and the Embassy Ambassador even allowed me to bury my dead bird George with full military honors (for a bird that meant a cigar box with an American flag) under a shade tree in his front yard. Unfortunately George literally reached for the heavens when the Embassy was bombed just six years later.

We moved almost every two years while my dad was in the Army: Louisiana, Germany, Virginia, Alabama, Kansas (three times), Maryland (two times), Kuwait and finally to Texas. My father had a stellar career and retired as a Lieutenant Colonel before working a full career at Boeing. I admire my mother's strength, grace and poise in supporting my father through many difficult assignments and military duties -

2

all while still maintaining her own interests and successes as the best mother in the world, a school teacher, real estate agent and cosmetics expert.

It was during our time in Kuwait that I learned the first of many valuable lessons about honesty. We spent a lot of time at the Embassy pool, especially in the summer. There was a snack bar and a group of "regular" ladies that sat on the edge of the pool with their feet in the water. There was also a baby pool where the youth gang played truth or dare, oblivious that the adults could see everything we were doing.

A small group of us signed up for the summer Swimming Contest; an "honor system" to write how many laps we swam each day on a large board posted at the pool area. I swam my little heart out that summer . . . every available moment spent doing laps. I had quite a lead on all the other contestants and I was determined that I would win, no matter what.

Then I started to notice that Sarah, one of the girls my age, had not only caught up with my lap number, but she was ahead of me. I didn't understand how that could happen because I never saw her swimming. While I was swimming laps, gulping gallons of water, she was playing with our gang of friends. When I asked her about it, she said she swam at night. It's true that she lived at the Embassy (one of only a few families – to include the Ambassador), but I was there in the eve-nings and still didn't see her swimming.

As the weeks went on I increased my efforts and swam even more laps, determined to win the contest. No matter how many laps I swam, I'd leave in the evening and the next day Sarah would have more than me.

I was talking to one of the "regular" ladies one night and told her how discouraged I was because no matter how many laps I swam, Sarah swam more. I wanted to win but I just couldn't swim any more laps per day . . . I was exhausted. This lady routinely stayed at the pool well into the night and told me that Sarah wasn't swimming laps. She had seen Sarah just write down numbers so she'd win.

I was angry and totally deflated. It didn't matter how much honest work I put into this . . . the girl that cheated and lied would win the trophy. When I got home, my mother and I had a long talk and I went to my bed and cried. When my father came in to talk to me, he said that he would not permit me to be in a contest with a liar and he was pulling me out of the competition. That upset me even more. Sarah was the one that should be removed so the rest of us had a fair compe-tition. I didn't lie so why did I have to leave? Dad would not hear of it. He didn't want me to be any part of an unfair competition and Sarah's parents should've taught their daughter not to lie. My parents felt it would send a valuable message that: 1) people knew I was the rightful winner – they had seen me swim the entire summer, and 2) I was withdrawn from the competition.

My parents bought me a beautiful First Place Swimmer's Trophy and it meant a lot to me . . . but to this day, that situation doesn't sit well. I understand that it was important to my parents that I withdraw from an unfair competition, but it's not right that I didn't take home the "real" trophy I earned. I wanted people to know the truth . . . that I was the winner and Sarah was a liar.

For all I know, people thought I got sick or broke a bone. I don't think it was clear to anyone what really happened and I'm sure Sarah never fessed up. I also don't know who Sarah's father was (in the political realm) but it may have been next to impossible to approach him about Sarah without my father committing career suicide.

As I look back to that event some 30 years ago, I realize that this world hasn't changed a bit. There are still liars and cheaters that seem to get the upper hand and take the "prize" . . . while others of us continue to work hard and tell the truth. What I can tell you is that it's still important. Honesty, truth and goodness may be rare commodities in today's culture but God and His requirements have never changed.

> *You shall not repeat or raise a false report; you shall not join with the wicked to be an unrighteous witness. You shall not follow a crowd to do evil; nor shall you bear witness at a trial so as to side with a multitude to pervert justice.*
> *Exodus 23:1-2 (AMP)*

> *To you who are ready for the truth, I say this: Love your enemies. Let them bring out the best in you, not the worst. When someone gives you a hard time, respond with the energies of prayer for that person. If someone slaps you in the face, stand there and take it. If someone grabs your shirt, gift wrap your best coat and make a present of it. If someone takes unfair advantage of you, use the occasion to practice the servant life. No more tit-for-tat stuff. Live generously. Luke 6:27-30 (MSG)*

Just as the following passage requires workers to respect authority, supervisors and/or those in positions of leadership will be held accountable for their actions:

> *Obey your leaders and submit to their authority. They keep watch over you <u>as men who must give an account</u>. Obey them*

so that their work will be a joy, not a burden, for that would be of no advantage to you. Hebrews 13:17 (NIV)

I've seen a lot of lying and cheating in my lifetime and I know I've done the right thing by taking the higher ground and turning the other cheek. I have and will continue to do that but this time it's important that people know what's going on. In regard to the FBI - the premier law enforcement agency in the world . . . it's time people know the truth! You will find the truth in these pages. To borrow the title of an old Clint Eastwood film, *The Good, the Bad and the Ugly.*

I'm not the first woman (nor person) to see the worst of the FBI and I'm sure I won't be the last. Even though it's difficult, I have to continue to stand up for what's right. I stood up in the FBI and got shot down. I'm standing up now and praying that God will use me to encourage and inspire others to keep getting up – to keep telling the truth – and to know that the Bible has already revealed the ending . . . the good guys win!

ﻉﻉﻉﻉﻉﻉﻉ

Let us not lose heart in doing good, for in due time we will reap if we do not grow weary. Galatians 6:9 (NAS)

ﻉﻉﻉﻉﻉﻉﻉ

Don't interfere with good people's lives; don't try to get the best of them. No matter how many times you trip them up, God-loyal people don't stay down long; Soon they're up on their feet, while the wicked end up flat on their faces. Proverbs 24:15-16 (TMB)

ﻉﻉﻉﻉﻉﻉﻉ

- All the events you are about to read are true but many names have been changed.

- To those who will see your malice on these pages, know that Satan used you well and by the grace of God I have forgiven you. I pray you will find that God is Bigger than the FBI or *anything* you will ever know. May God bless you and put you on His path and may you not cause any more harm.

∾ 1 ∾

The FBI Motto

Fidelity, Bravery, Integrity

"People do not like to think. If one thinks, one must reach conclusions. Conclusions are not always pleasant." ~ Helen Keller

∾∾∾∾∾∾∾

The FBI is the premier law enforcement agency in the world - or so they say. I still haven't figured out who "they" are.

I was an FBI Special Agent (SA) for nine years. I was told that distinction elevated me to be the top 2% of the population. After all, it's harder to be appointed as an FBI SA than it is to be accepted into Harvard. That's just the beginning of the Bluff-n-Stuff (BS) "they" say.

As for me, I believed (and still do) in the FBI Motto, I believed in the exceptional work done by the FBI (that I read about and saw in news reports), and I spent my life developing and living what the FBI claims to hold so dear.

Before you plot a course, go on a trip or make a journey, it's important to know your starting point. For my journey with the FBI, I started with the FBI Seal, FBI Motto and FBI Core Values. Please take a moment to really understand what is meant by the words chosen to represent the FBI. I've outlined them below and they will help you understand why I often felt alone and faced challenges and difficulties in upholding these ideals through my FBI journey.

FBI SEAL

Each symbol and color in the FBI seal has special significance. The dominant blue field of the seal and the scales on the shield represent justice. The endless circle of 13 stars denotes unity of purpose as exemplified by the original 13 states. The laurel leaf has, since early civilization, symbolized academic honors, distinction and fame. There are exactly 46 leaves in the two branches, since there were 46 states in the Union when the FBI was founded in 1908. The significance of the red and white parallel stripes lies in their colors. Red traditionally stands for courage, valor, strength, while white conveys cleanliness, light, truth, and peace. As in the American Flag, the red bars exceed the white by one. The motto, "Fidelity, Bravery, Integrity," succinctly describes the motivating force behind the men and women of the FBI. The peaked bevelled edge which circumscribes the seal symbolizes the severe challenges confronting the FBI and the ruggedness of the organization. The gold color in the seal conveys its over-all value.

www.fbi.gov/libref/historic/fbiseal/fbiseal.htm

FBI MOTTO
FIDELITY, BRAVERY, INTEGRITY

FIDELITY

Faithfulness to something to which one is bound by pledge or duty:
ALLEGIANCE, FEALTY, LOYALTY, DEVOTION, PIETY
FIDELITY - strict and continuing faithfulness to an obligation, trust, or duty
ALLEGIANCE - adherence like that of citizens to their country
FEALTY - fidelity acknowledged by the individual and as compelling as a sworn vow
LOYALTY - faithfulness that is steadfast in the face of any temptation to renounce, desert, or betray
DEVOTION - zeal and service amounting to self-dedication
PIETY - fidelity to obligations regarded as natural and fundamental
Accuracy in details: EXACTNESS

BRAVERY

Mental or moral strength to venture, persevere, and withstand danger, fear, or difficulty; and to resist opposition, danger, or hardship: COURAGE, METTLE, SPIRIT, RESOLUTION, TENACITY
COURAGE - firmness of mind and will in the face of danger or extreme difficulty <the *courage* to support unpopular causes>
METTLE - ingrained capacity for meeting strain or difficulty with fortitude and resilience
SPIRIT - a quality of temperament enabling one to hold one's own or keep up one's morale when opposed or threatened <her *spirit* was unbroken>
RESOLUTION – firm determination to achieve one's ends
TENACITY adds to RESOLUTION implications of stubborn persistence and unwillingness to admit defeat <held to their beliefs with great *tenacity*>.

INTEGRITY

Firm adherence to a code of especially moral or artistic values: INCORRUPTIBILITY
SOUNDNESS - an unimpaired condition
COMPLETENESS - the quality or state of being complete or undivided: **synonym** see HONESTY
Uprightness of character or action.
HONESTY - refusal to lie, steal, or deceive in any way
HONOR - active or anxious regard for the standards of one's profession, calling, or position.
INTEGRITY - trustworthiness and incorruptibility to a degree that one is incapable of being false to a trust, responsibility, or pledge
PROBITY - tried and proven honesty or integrity
Merriam-Webster Online: www.m-w.com

FBI CORE VALUES

The FBI will strive for excellence in all aspects of its missions. In pursuing these missions and vision, the FBI and its employees will be true to, and exemplify, the following core values:

- Adherence to the rule of law and the rights conferred to all under the United States Constitution;
- Integrity through everyday ethical behavior;
- Accountability by accepting responsibility for our actions and decisions and the consequences of our actions and decisions;
- Fairness in dealing with people; and
- Leadership through example, both at work and in our communities.

www.fbi.gov/priorities/priorities.htm

Doesn't that sound great? I actually believed it to be true. I never expected the FBI would be perfect, every organization has its challenges, but I did expect to find individuals striving for excellence. Unfortunately, what I discovered was that all that "stuff" was only window dressing. It seems that those valiant words are written strictly for shirt emblems, websites, school children, applicants, the American people and Congress – not for those inside the walls of the FBI. I should've had a hint of things to come when our class was notified of the FBI Director's "Bright Line" Policy during training at Quantico.

> *Director Louis Freeh's "Bright Line" Policy:*
> *January 1994 – the "simple truth that lying, cheating, or stealing is wholly inconsistent with everything the FBI stands for and cannot be tolerated." Lying under oath, voucher fraud, theft, and material falsification of investigative activity or reporting- are examples of behavior for which employees could expect to be dismissed.*
> www.usdoj.gov/oig/special/0211/chapter6.htm

At the time it didn't occur to me how significant it was that the FBI Director wrote this policy. The "Bright Line" would not be necessary unless there were rampant problems. Why do you have to remind your FBI SAs not to lie, cheat or steal? Just think about how prevalent the problems must be if the FBI Director has to make a "policy" to effect *change* in these areas and distribute it throughout the FBI. These issues were woven into the institutional fabric of the FBI throughout the entire nation.

It's still difficult for me to come to terms with the fact that most people in my New Agents Class (NAC), for that matter most individuals throughout the FBI started out as "good" people. They had to be good . . . right? After all, the FBI does in-depth testing, background investigations and even a polygraph (lie detector) test before acceptance. Only the best of the best make it into the FBI. So where does the shift occur that turns these "good" individuals from the outside . . . into liars, cheaters and thieves once they get in.

I believe it starts at the FBI Academy. The FBI makes it very clear that whatever you did in your previous life doesn't matter - in fact *you* really didn't matter . . . before. Any outstanding skills, talents or abilities you may have brought with you are summarily dismissed in light of what really matters . . . that *now* you've "arrived;" *now* you're somebody; *now* you're an FBI Special Agent.

When we got to the FBI Academy, I think we were all anxious to learn and absorbed knowledge . . . like sponges. We learned very valuable information. We also learned to do what we were told and that once all this [training] was over, we'd be in the elite and exclusive club of "Special Agents." Along with the academics, firearms, physical training and practical applications, we were also learning to keep silent and embrace drunkenness, disrespect and inappropriate sexual behavior. Make no mistake, the FBI's true culture is taught and re-enforced well at the Academy.

Every new agent class has two class counselors at Quantico. We had a great one - Ben, and an awful one - Paul. Ben was a seasoned professional interested in helping each and every one of us. He told interesting FBI stories that we listened to intently, he had a quick wit and a warm and engaging personality. He was a living example for "the best of the best." I remember one evening when most of the class was out on the town, I stayed behind worried about an upcoming White Collar Crime exam. Ben ensured that I was ready by quizzing me until I felt confident and prepared.

If you were to interview every single NAC 97-10 class member, you'd likely find that Ben took the time to help each person in some special way.

Paul was the complete opposite . . . a crabby, arrogant old man with a bad attitude. He was more concerned with strutting around trying to impress us lowly students by acting "cool" than he was in helping anyone. He enjoyed belittling us at every opportunity and we stayed as far away from him as possible. True to form, he only got angrier as he saw the class warm to Ben and further distance from him. Paul also made it a point to tell us that once we graduated, we'd be let in on "the best kept secret in the FBI." Of course we were all curious but he never fully explained himself. As I think back to his cryptic comments I realize that he was talking about what the FBI internally refers to as "ballooning" (going up, up and away – never to be seen) or "banging the books."

There's an often repeated joke about three little boys trying to "top" each other bragging about their fathers. The first little boy said as a cop, his dad left before he got up in the morning, gave traffic tickets and drove around the city keeping everyone safe all day. He came home after the little boy was in bed. The second little boy said as a Drug Enforcement Administration (DEA) agent, his dad left before he got up in the morning, put dangerous drug dealers in jail but was usually home to say goodnight just before the little boy went to sleep - except on the weekends when he never saw his dad. The third little boy said that as an FBI agent, his dad ate breakfast with him every day, took him to school and visited with the teachers, solved the best cases in the country, chaperoned the fun school field trips, coached his soccer team, ate dinner with him and tucked him in bed each night. He had a "super dad" because on top of all that, his dad told him to say that he works 16 hours a day. I never thought it was a very good joke either. The point is that a *lot* of FBI agents "bang the books." They lie on their federal time registers without any consequences and they are not held responsible for FBI work.

That's the best kept secret Paul was talking about. Once we got our credentials we joined the ranks of the few people in the country who would be well respected, have almost unlimited power with unlimited freedom – be paid well and not have to do . . . anything.

You will see the FBI at its best in times of crisis and high profile cases – especially and primarily if the media is involved. That's when working SAs come together to get the job done . . . and it's an incredible thing when it happens! Those are the things I read so much about before I joined the FBI . . . and they are the things that you will still read about. However, those are neither the things at the core of the FBI nor what happens on a daily basis inside the FBI walls.

I'll give you just two (of too many to count) examples of the best kept secret. The first in Albuquerque with an agent I'll call Greg. He married a female agent and exposed me to the "Cubicle Bomb" I'll talk about later.

FBI policy clearly states that Special Agents are to work an average of 10 hours per day for each year period. This equates to eight "regular" hours per day plus two hours of Administratively Uncontrollable Overtime (AUO) for a 50 hour workweek (by the way, most agents don't even know what AUO means). By "average" it is understood that some weeks may be 40 hours and some 80 hours but by year end you must average (at least) 50 hours per week. The AUO is in place to compensate agents for the excessive overtime <u>expected</u> to be involved with investigating our nation's federal crimes. With a constant backlog of cases, there is enough work in the FBI for every agent to be busy around the clock.

As with everything in the FBI, there is a policy and the AUO policy absolutely excludes agent commute time. Though many agents justified and argued that they were "on the clock" the moment they left their residence and got in their FBI cars with their FBI radios and FBI guns - the FBI clearly states that FBI SA sign-in time is to reflect the actual time <u>working</u>. Because of AUO, we were paid an additional 25% of our base salary. Even for the new agents, this meant an additional ~ $11,000 per year and senior agents added ~ $25,000 per year for their extra two hours per day. AUO was put in effect to compensate the elite FBI SA workforce for the hard work and sacrifice made to our country.

Years ago (before my time) I was told that agents were on very short leashes and had to do "stupid" things like . . . come to the office and sign in before they did anything outside the office. They were also required to physically come to the office to sign out at the end of the day. As time moved forward, agents were considered "trustworthy" so they would just call the secretary to report their time - or go days without reporting at all. With "honor system" reporting, agents could meet a source or go on an operation without having to stop by the office first. Rather than recognize this as a way to assist agents in their duties and time management, many identified it as an easy way to manipulate and cheat the system. It reminds me of the Kuwait Swimming Contest with Sarah that I discussed in the Introduction.

We're talking about the FBI here - FBI SAs - you know, the people you thought were honest and trustworthy? In the FBI, where there's a will (and a pen) . . . there's a way. Greg and his wife had over an hour commute to the Albuquerque office. Greg and I were White Collar Crime Squad-mates as well as cubicle-mates. We often got to the office at the same time and took the elevator together. I'd stop by my desk to drop off my briefcase and purse and then sign in at the secretary's desk. Greg signed in just minutes before I did . . . at 6:30 a.m. – but the actual time was 8:15 a.m. (and the time I signed in). I also noticed that he left the office no later than 5:00 yet he signed his time register that he worked until 6:30. In other words, while I stayed to literally work until 7:00 p.m. because that was my job, Greg was "banging the books" three hours per day. That equates to 15 hours per week, 780 hours per year – or 19 1/2 weeks (almost five months) that you, the taxpayers, paid Greg's salary and he did absolutely nothing but drive to and from work – using gas and a car fully paid by the FBI! Even considering only AUO, not wasted time that I'll talk about later – this single agent over the course of his 20 year career will "steal" over 390 weeks, seven and a half (7 ½) years of salary from you.

Everyone on the squad knew what Greg did (including the supervisor) but nothing was ever said because most of the agents were doing the same thing. That's another FBI trait that made me sick to my stomach. Agents would bait fellow agents to get down and dirty so they all had "something" on each other. No one could speak up about any wrongdoing for fear that they'd be caught themselves.

I'm not suggesting that every agent lies. There are hard working agents at every level but I can tell you that I was absolutely shocked by the number of agents that, with clear conscience, considered banging the books to be a simple FBI perk that no one challenged. If an agent wanted to come in late or leave early they would just "disappear" or say they were "checking a lead" – which was agent lingo for "I'm out of here. Don't call me."

The second example involves Fred, a former supervisor in the Houston FBI office. That's an important distinction because the "FBI Boys Club" got more intimate and bullet proof with each step up the supervisory ladder. Fred was quite an unremarkable man. I don't know how he ever advanced to the level of supervisor but he took more and more advantage with his position.

He was finally caught with help by the local media. Apparently Fred had been an outstanding kids' sports coach (using several hours in the middle of the day) for years. The reporter that covered Fred's great philanthropic efforts was unaware that Fred had been doing dou-ble-duty. While Fred was being heralded for his mid-day service with the kids, Fred was officially being paid for his expertise to lead a squad as an FBI supervisor, all the time lying to his superiors. Direc-tor Freeh's "Bright Line" policy addressed these issues and stated that employees could expect to be dismissed for such actions . . . so Fred was dismissed right? I'm sure you're way ahead of me . . . the rules don't apply to the "Boys Club!" In fact if the news coverage had been the only "evidence" it's unlikely that anything would've happened to Fred. Only because a secretary (not agents) refused to lie about Fred's actions when she was questioned, was Fred "severely punished." He was demoted to a senior agent and requested a transfer to San Juan.

The world would be truly amazed at what the FBI could accom-plish if the entire FBI SA population were required to "work." This will remain the "best kept secret in the FBI" - to steal your money - until you require change! (No pun intended)

I experienced, and saw others experience, the senior agent FBI in-doctrination into the field office. This boiled down to new agents, extremely talented and experienced professionals, being "broken down" and treated like morons.

I quickly identified a consistent phenomenon I called the "two month window." From the time a new agent came to the field office, there was a period of two months before a palpable choice was made to: 1) take the high road by doing the right thing - working and having a positive attitude, or 2) sinking in the mud pit of mediocrity and de-ception where the majority of agents rooted.

"The high minded man must care more for the truth than for what people think." ~ Aristotle

❧ 2 ❧

The Beginning

"Take a chance! All life is a chance. The man who goes the furthest is generally the one who is willing to do and dare." ~ Dale Carnegie

❧❧❧❧❧❧

Until 1996, I had never encountered a real FBI Special Agent. Not many people have, or will . . . well, not many of the "good guys" anyway. And why should you, there are only about 12,000 FBI SAs and they mostly inbreed in their social interactions.

Oh, I'd seen them on TV and thought all the cops and robbers shoot-'em-ups were exciting. I even took the public tour of the FBI Headquarters building in Washington, DC when I was working as a Public/Customer Relations Specialist for TRW, a Government Contractor for Ballistic Missile Defense Systems. You'd think that at the very least the FBI tour, full of mystery and intrigue would ignite some hidden desire. Nope! I went right on working with Pentagon and other high level officials.

My interest in the FBI was piqued during a visit to Colorado with my sister Natalie. I wanted to make a difference with my life. I wanted to help people, to serve and to impact my country in a positive way - I just didn't know how.

Natalie and I toured the Air Force Academy and saw the visitor's film. As an Army brat reared on military Posts, there's awareness I can almost taste when I enter a military facility - warmth and familiarity that I'm where I belong. I felt that sense of belonging sitting there in the dark theater at the Air Force Academy, absorbing every image and patriotic symbol. The film was obviously designed to ignite passion and American pride and it did an outstanding job in those areas. My spirit sank when it was over and I told Natalie that I really missed the mark by not going with my original life-goal to be an Air Force Nurse. I felt my opportunity to serve my country had passed me by and I was too old to go down that path.

Natalie has a special gift of encouragement and has always been one of my greatest cheerleaders. She assured me that at age 31, I still had ample opportunity to make a difference in this world. She planted the seed for me to join the FBI.

My first thought was, "Yeah right, they let women in the FBI." Then I learned that women were first allowed in the FBI as Special Agents in 1972 – of course, after J. Edgar Hoover was dead and buried. The wooing of women to the FBI Special Agent position will be discussed in Chapter 11 – *Women Need Not Apply.*

I was given the opportunity to speak with married FBI agents in California and I also cold-called the FBI office in Colorado Springs and asked to speak to a female SA. I was transferred to SA Raynol and after explaining my interest in getting more information, apart from any recruiter pitch, she agreed to meet me for lunch. When I returned to Alabama, another cold-call resulted in meeting SA Yunge. These women were extremely professional, articulate, had great personalities and most impressive to me – they had an ease about them. They were comfortable in their skin. I remember being very inspired by each of them.

I was working as a Marketing Consultant for the Huntsville International Airport at that time. Betty, a talented and spunky executive, offered to introduce me to Carl, a retired Special Agent in Charge (SAC – the highest position within each FBI Field Office). He had worked in the Birmingham FBI office and now lived in Huntsville.

I appreciated the opportunity to meet a "high" official from the FBI and I have to give Betty the benefit of the doubt because Carl was only an "acquaintance" to her. That said, I met Carl for lunch and had numerous questions that he patiently answered. He was charming and entertaining, and he enjoyed impressing me with all his FBI stories. He even wrote a very nice letter of recommendation for my background investigation. I'm afraid that's all the good I can say.

Carl was an aging man with an active libido for younger women - me at that time. I was quite naïve and didn't immediately recognize the "slimy moves" being volleyed at me. He took quite an interest in meeting with me for more discussions, always sure to say it would give me more information about the FBI. I was very flattered and felt quite special that he would take an interest in my career and my aspirations to become an FBI SA. I thought this was a "what goes around comes around" time for me. I often spoke with "younger" folks . . . assisting them with career advice, job fairs or motivational presentations. Now Carl was helping me in my career - or so I thought!

Even with my consistent resistance and attempts to keep things professional and centered on the FBI, Carl continued to make me very uncomfortable with his constant compliments and "lingering" hugs (Yuk). I just dismissed them. After all, he was over 20 years older than me, surely he wasn't thinking of me like "that."

One of my very wise girlfriends, Katie, informed me that Carl had a "reputation" and his latest ex-wife was several years younger than me . . . Unbelievable! I sincerely hoped that wasn't the case and that he wasn't "putting the moves on me." That question was clearly answered when he invited me on a "trip to the country" where a lot of "very powerful people would be gathering." He said he'd introduce me to high level FBI personnel and even Attorney General Janet Reno. He insisted it would help my chances of getting into the FBI if I knew more people on the inside.

I may be naïve and gullible – but I'm not an idiot! I felt slimy even having the conversation with him so I ended that meeting as soon as possible. He was relentless in his follow up about this offer . . . sweetening the deal by saying what fun I'd have riding horses, etc.

I'll either be accepted or denied by the FBI on my own merit - not by being a wannabe, hanging out with this guy. I could only imagine what Janet Reno would say about that. I doubt it would be anything positive and I would definitely not be seen as a serious, professional, FBI candidate.

I'm still disgusted that Carl tried to manipulate me to get involved with him by playing on my desire for a professional career in the FBI. I dismissed the entire thing as a sad old man and a bad FBI seed. Surely he was not the norm . . . or was he?

❧❧❧❧❧❧

"Knowledge without wisdom is a load of books on the back of an ass." ~ Japanese Proverb

~3~

Getting In

"Freedom means the opportunity to be what we never thought we would be." ~ Daniel Joseph Boorstin

~~~~~~

The FBI application process is long and difficult - in every area you can imagine. I understand they only accept applications on-line these days and the entire process and all requirements can be found at www.fbijobs.gov.

If after reading this book and conducting your own research you are still interested in applying to the FBI as a Special Agent, be committed to the process, be patient and be prepared to hurry up and wait. I've given you my experience and timeline below:

STEP 1: THE SHORT APPLICATION
3/13/1996

This is very much like a regular job application with basic information. I sent it in and waited. I also prayed that I would only be accepted if it was what God wanted for me. My parents had concerns about the safety aspect of being an FBI Special Agent. After all, FBI agents carry guns and arrest people . . . and I'm their baby girl. However, I know that anything that happens to me has to go through God's hands first. I accepted Jesus as my Lord and Savior when I was 13 years old so I'm ready to be with Him any time He wants me.

When I told my brother Jeff about my application – he invited me over to his house. Jeff is a big guy. He's the cool, tough "man's man" that girls always went crazy for. In fact, while we were growing up there were a lot of girls that befriended me just to get to him. Jeff was in college ROTC and had many years of martial arts training. If anyone in our family were to be an FBI agent, we'd all expect it to be him. And if you were wondering, he's off the market - happily married to Stacy for 18 years with three beautiful children. As I was walking across his lawn, Jeff met me mid-way with that brotherly tone, "Sooo - you're gonna be in the FBI huh!?" With that, he did some crazy martial arts move that flipped me upside down and left me flat on my back seeing sky – of course with him standing over me grinning. I told him to go ahead and pick on me now because once I became an agent he'd be "assaulting a Federal Officer." We both had a good laugh. He was excited for me and very supportive of my new adventure. In fact my entire family has supported me and prayed for me throughout each step of my FBI journey.

Once I put in my application, I hit the gym - - - Gold's gym. I worked out six days per week with cardio and strength training and I started doing the things required for the FBI Physical Fitness test; push-ups, pull-ups, sit-ups, sprints and runs. I've never enjoyed running . . . even on the tennis team in high school and college I got very good at placing shots so I'd keep my opponent on the run rather than me. Since then I've said that if you see me running, look for the guy chasing me trying to steal my purse. As much as I disliked it - I learned to do it pretty well - with a lot of help from an amazing man - Big John Shropshire.

Big John was a phenomenal trainer . . . a 300 pound black man with a smile that lit up city blocks. We'd met years earlier in a step-aerobics class where he was blasting his whistle and barking (like a dog) to get people motivated. He absolutely cracked me up and I turned around and barked back at him. It gave a whole new meaning to "Who let the dogs out?!" Our barking antics led to a deep friendship and when I told him that I applied to the FBI, he offered to train me at no cost. Big John's motto was, "I can motivate a rock" and he never faltered from his commitment to me or anyone else in lifting spirits and moving people beyond limitations they put on themselves.

The gym was located at the end of a small retail mall and Big John made arrangements for us to practice the FBI shuttle run in the middle of the mall after closing. It was incredible how his big voice boomed and echoed and I can still hear him in my mind encouraging me to keep pushing. Big John did several fitness videos for Reebok on Fit TV, a series of videos for Time Life Medical, an ABC 20/20 segment on fitness coming in all sizes, and was the co-host/instructor of AL TV

"Step-n-Style" (www.rsports.com/hsf/Aerobics/johnshro.htm). After a distinguished military career, he was at the brink of taking the fitness world by storm.

Big John and I had a loving friendship and we made each other laugh. He often referred to me as an angel on earth and being with him made me feel protected, loved and special. Time with him also got me in really good shape and prepared me for the FBI training. He was so proud when I graduated from the FBI Academy and brought him memorabilia. Three months later, at age 43, Big John went to be with the Lord.

I still can't go to a gym without thinking of him and I've never gotten over Big John's passing in regard to working out. I've had short memberships at several gyms through the years but I haven't stayed long. I know Big John would kick my rear for that but it's still painful and the loss is revived when I go to places connected to my dear friend. I miss him.

STEP 2: PHASE I TESTING
6/12/1996

I was so excited the FBI wanted me to continue through the application process. They are seeking "competitive" candidates and I had no idea if I was one - or even what that meant. The FBI's definition of "competitive" changes from year to year. One year they may want attorneys, then accountants, then computer experts, then language specialists, then proven leaders. I have two years of Nursing and a Bachelor of Science degree in Business Administration with a minor in Management Information Systems. There's no way to figure out what the FBI wants - - - they don't know what they want, nor when they want it.

Over the years, many high school and college students have asked me what they should study and major in to become an FBI SA. My answer is always the same - study what you enjoy and concentrate on areas that support your passion. There is never a guarantee that you will be accepted into the FBI and you need to prepare for a successful career in an area that you really enjoy. It was very sad to come across (mostly men) that dreamed of being an FBI SA since they were young, majored in Criminal Justice (though they didn't enjoy it) and then didn't pass one of the FBI testing phases and were lost in where to go from there.

I found that the FBI is not necessarily interested in Criminal Justice majors. It makes sense if you understand the FBI culture. As the "premier law enforcement agency in the world" the FBI is a stand alone agency that prides itself with doing things independently, without checks and balances and only the way "they" want.

Criminal Justice majors have an edge in learning how things "should" be done regarding the law and law enforcement agencies. It follows then that the FBI would be wary in allowing candidates through the door that would identify their problems and try to "correct" them. Inside the walls of the FBI I often heard that "they" weren't interested in Criminal Justice majors because the students had no "real" education. The same was often said of candidates coming from other law enforcement agencies such as police departments. I was only aware of a few that made it through and became SAs.

I also noticed around 2002 that more and more new agents were coming from a military background. I wondered why there was a shift in welcoming them since when I arrived in the late 90's, they were often overlooked. When I became an SA, the focus for an SA candidate was on proven ability and leadership. The shift I witnessed may have started with the terrorist attacks of 9/11. It seemed that the FBI started seeking followers, not leaders.

I have full respect and admiration for our military men and women that provide outstanding service to our country. They allow us to claim our freedom through their sacrifice. My comments here are about the make up of a good "young" individual in military service. That is, the ability to follow orders without question or hesitation. That is a trait that may save lives in battles and wars.

However, true leadership and the ability to make difficult decisions requires free thinking individuals who can distinguish true wisdom, follow only knowledgeable leaders, question poor decisions and have the ability to inspire, encourage and lead others. The skill set required of leaders is very different than that of followers. The FBI has suffered because of poor management due to the shift away from bringing in great leaders. Unfortunately, these followers are often quickly promoted to management positions without the skills or knowledge to achieve FBI organizational goals and objectives. They rise up because they follow so well. That does not make them capable of leadership. Couple that with immaturity and the complete lack of FBI management training and you have what you see today . . . an FBI suffering from inexcusable and ridiculous blunders.

Even now, FBI Director Robert Mueller is defending FBI agents before Congress for breaking the law regarding the Patriot Act.

> *In a review of headquarters files and a sampling of four of the FBI's 56 field offices, Inspector General Glenn A. Fine found* **48 violations of law or presidential directives** *during 2003-2005. He estimates there may be as many as 3,000 violations throughout the FBI that have not been identified or reported.*
> www.cbsnews.com/stories/2007/03/27/terror/main2613379.shtml

Director Muller takes full responsibility saying, "The statute did not cause the errors. The FBI's implementation did." Only the arrogance of the FBI could produce a "leader" that excuses sworn FBI agents breaking the law, and then in the same breath, claim to enforce the laws of our nation. The hypocrisy is dumbfounding. How far do you think you'd get in robbing a bank for the just cause of feeding your family and then telling the police officers that it was only a mistake and there should be no adverse action? Mueller should've been laughed out of his chair. The truly sad reality is that there was no laughter.

All that said, the Phase I testing was a three part - written, multiple choice, timed test given at the Birmingham Field Office processing my application. The first and third sections were very similar and as instructed, I just told it like it was. Many questions were "what if's" regarding various situations. Because it's timed, I had to move very quickly with little time to ponder my answers. I went with my first instinct and moved on. The middle section is math - very difficult math. I prepared for the test by working through every SAT study guide I could find. I had been out of college and the whole "testing" mode for quite some time so I needed help to get back up to speed. The study process helped me tremendously.

It was amusing that the sample test booklet the FBI gave me had simple questions like 2+6-3 = 5. The actual test involved fuel capacities and propulsion formulas. It was bizarre.

NOTIFIED OF PASSING PHASE I
6/18/1996

STEP 3: THE LONG APPLICATION
6/27/1996

You might as well take a week off work to get this done. It took me 40 hours to complete the application. It required "detail" to say the least. From my Army family roots to relocating after college I had moved 24 times and it took a great deal of research just to find the residential information they requested (old addresses, dates, neighbors, etc.) not to mention the 13 employers I had with supervisors, dates, salary information, etc. Those positions included: Lifeguard (for the largest wave-pool theme park in the US), Daycare Center Teacher, Grocery Store Traveling Cashier (throughout the Southwest), Bartender, Retail Clerk, Waitress, Office Administrator, Public Relations Director, Actress, Marketing, Advertising and finally at the Aerospace company TRW, entering at a low level position and promoting to be the Public and Customer Relations Specialist for Ballistic Missile Defense Systems (BMDS) – Huntsville, Alabama and Washington, DC. A separate page was required to identify my special skills and supervisory experience. I think the only things not listed were babysitting and Burger King.

I also had to provide all my family information (to include addresses, dates of birth, Social Security Numbers, etc.), references, educational history, foreign travel (with passport information), organization memberships, tickets and court cases, all financial information, any relatives employed by the government, any friends or acquaintances of the FBI and your first born child (just kidding on the last one).

As frustrating as it was, I knew it was only the beginning of my career in digging for details. Even then, it was very obvious to me that things get missed if you rush or cut corners. To get the entire story, you need details.

I also went to Birmingham to talk with the FBI recruiter in person. I didn't want to join the FBI unless I was a good fit for them and they were a good fit for me. There was no reason to waste each others time. I was not a tough guy man-chic and had no interest in becoming one. My interest was in finding a rewarding career where my talents and skills would be utilized to the fullest and still be able to have a personal life.

Supervisory Special Agent (SSA) Deela assured me that there was no agent "mold" I needed to fit and he had just returned from his honeymoon so there was definitely time for a personal life outside the FBI. He also explained the FBI's 10 year part-time program often used by female agents raising children. Since my desire was to have a career and a family, I thought this was the perfect fit . . . and it wouldn't be a bad thing if I were to meet Mr. Right among the SAs. After all, we'd understand the demands of the job and could actually talk to each other since we'd both have *Top Secret* Clearances.

STEP 4: PHASE II TESTING/INTERVIEW
10/29/1996 - Ft. Lauderdale, FL

After the FBI reviewed my long application, I was notified that I was moving on to Phase II. I remember this as the first time it felt "real" to me and I was starting to get excited about becoming an SA. The FBI avoids all appearances of applicant favoritism (in case you might know someone from your local office) so each candidate is sent to another geographical area for Phase II. I was flown to Ft. Lauderdale for the two-part testing: a three person panel interview and a report writing exercise.

I was in a group of about twelve and I remember the facilitator offering encouragement to help calm us down. The most important point he made, "Do not throw up in front of the interview panel."

Six of us would go through the interview process first, with the others completing the report phase. I was to be interviewed first. When I walked in the room, one of the men looked at me in surprise and said they were expecting a man. I looked at him with a straight face and stated in a very serious tone, "I used to be a man." We all laughed, he winked and then said I had a really good doctor. That's actually not something to joke about now-a-days. Houston is home to a transgender SA that joined the FBI as a man and is now a woman.

My name has the spelling most often used by males so it was good to know that I had not received any special treatment or placement in the FBI testing phases because I was a female. I got through each phase based on my qualifications, skills and abilities. That's very unlike one woman who told her interview panel that she was gay, living an alternate lifestyle and if she didn't get in . . . she would make problems for the FBI.

The interview is quite intense. They tape recorded the entire process and each of the three SAs asked questions in rotation. They find out what you're made of. In "active" listening you receive constant feedback by the listener giving verbal and non-verbal cues. For example, nodding your head with understanding, or saying "ah huh" or making an expression of question or disapproval - you get the idea. What I remember most about this interview was seeing the top of each persons head. They gave no verbal or non-verbal listening cues. In fact, they gave no response at all - they simply wrote notes the entire time - except for the man in front of me that kicked me under the table three different times. The third time, I asked if he was trying to tell me something. He just laughed and apologized.

Being an actress has distinct advantages in a number of situations. My inner dialog during this interview was that I must be saying things that are so great they have to write them down. In doing that, my energy was higher at the end of the hour than when I arrived. I answered all the questions thoughtfully and honestly and felt very confident that it went well.

I've since learned that the majority of candidates don't make it through this interview stage. I think these folks go in expecting positive feedback and when they don't get it, they sink back.

Here's the thing . . . as an FBI SA out on the streets, people look to you to solve whatever problem is at hand - be it a bank robbery, arrest, interview . . . whatever. You don't get positive feedback - you often get resistance and chaos. It's important to have the inner strength to "bring it" when you have to rely on yourself in difficult and even dangerous situations. This interview process is only a tiny example of what's to come and I think it's a good measure of who's got "it."

The report writing was straight forward and again, I think it's a good measure of things to come since the entire FBI is based on documentation and reports. It was simply an exercise in organizing content, developing an outline and writing in a clear and concise manner. Having seen some horrendous reports written by current agents, I believe this phase of the testing should carry more weight and hinder more candidates from moving on.

NOTIFIED OF PASSING PHASE II
11/7/1996

STEP 5: POLYGRAPH AND DRUG TESTING
11/20/1996

I was very nervous about the polygraph (lie detector) test. Not because I planned to lie, but because I didn't know if they were really accurate. What if I told the truth and the machine said I lied? As people got word that I was going through FBI testing, many made it a point to tell me all the bad stories about their "friend" that failed . . . or about the bad polygraphers . . . or about their Uncle Joe that never told a lie in his life – but failed the polygraph. I don't know what happened in those cases but I was told by FBI agents in Huntsville that you can't fail a polygraph test if you tell the truth. Well, I can follow direction so I told the polygrapher everything I'd done since the third grade.

We even had a little tiff in the pre-interview. He asked if I ever consistently lied about anything and I told him, "Yes." He perked up to hear the details. I told him that if a man asks me out on a date and I'm not interested, I may tell him I'm involved with someone or have plans – even if that's not the case. He told me I should never do that. I should tell the men that I'm not interested and why I feel that way. I questioned why I should knowingly hurt someone's feelings if I'm not interested in them. Then I thought to myself, "Don't argue with the guy doing your test." I told him I'd consider his input. Since then I have considered what he said and we were both right - - - and wrong. I should be honest and say I'm not interested but I don't have to give an explanation. There's no reason to shoot down anyone by criticizing them . . . their beliefs, looks, job, ambition, body-odor, whatever it is. They don't need me to dent their self-esteem when they are the ideal *Prince Charming* for another woman.

I had stitches in my finger from a cut I got when a waitress dropped a tray of glasses on me and the polygrapher said he had to put the machine contact on that finger. I've since learned that *he* was lying - he could've used a different finger. But I just let it throb away and went through the polygraph . . . for two and a half hours.

26

When it was over, the polygrapher went into another room to look at the results. He told me that it still had to be verified by FBI Headquarters but it appeared as though I passed. I tilted my head, remained very calm and quietly asked if I could do my "Happy Dance." I saw the first glimpse of a grin on his face since I walked in the door. He hesitated for a moment and then with a full smile said, "Sure." I was sitting down but my body was doing a full dance while I sang, "Oh happy . . . oh happy." His demeanor instantly changed and he became very warm and said he wasn't nearly the jerk I must think he is. I didn't think he was a jerk, he was doing his job - and being very serious about it. No problem!

STEP 6: PHYSICAL EXAM
12/09/1996

This is general testing and poking to make sure you won't break.
* Be sure to review the FBI vision requirements.

NOTIFICATION FOR QUANTICO
2/14/1997 TO REPORT ON 3/2/1997

The call came while I was sleeping. I was visiting Natalie in Colorado and she made a special parchment scroll for me with the FBI news. I wasn't even fully awake when we both started screaming and jumping up and down – it was a great celebration to share together. She was also with me when I made a big personal sacrifice . . . cutting off my fingernails. Natalie is a list maker and she started right away with who to call, things I'd need, what I needed to do, you name it - it was on the list - and that list was extremely helpful. She's also great at encouragement through cards and notes. Natalie was on a campaign to lift me up and help me through the difficult training to come and her support meant the world to me.

My friends from Whitesburg Baptist Church threw me a surprise going away party complete with fake badges, radios, sunglasses and ear pieces – I never knew my friends could look so cool. We had a great time and I was so touched that they would go to that effort to wish me well and kick off the new FBI chapter of my life.

My entire family and all my friends rallied around me. They let me know they were proud of me and they encouraged me throughout training. They also made it clear that the FBI was lucky to be getting me. I felt loved and thanked God for getting me that far.

TIPS FOR FBI PHASE II TESTING

1) They don't know what you don't tell them. They may not review your resume before they see you so be sure and include all the good stuff you've done. It's not bragging if you don't get arrogant. Be confident and tell them the facts . . . especially the really <u>great</u> stuff!

2) A lot of folks start off well and then go down hill. The panel will not be active listeners - probably won't give eye contact, head nods, etc. Just think that every time they write something down (which they do throughout the interview) - you said something soooo great they didn't want to forget it. End on the same or higher note and energy than where you started.

3) Don't waste time! If something doesn't come to you right away, skip to the next question and they'll come back to it if there's time at the end.

4) Make sure each "story" or "example" you give has a beginning, middle and end. What was the situation, what did you do about it and what was the outcome? Try to use examples where you played a major leadership role - not just observed as a bystander.

5) The written exam will determine if you can organize information and report it logically. I did an outline before I started writing my paper so I could keep it on track. Use all the time you're given. Even if you get finished early - don't leave. Keep reviewing your paper. I was the last one out of the room when they called "time." I noticed a lot of the other people didn't make it through.

6) For goodness sake . . . don't listen to any other applicants that are in your interviewing group - they have no idea what's going on and if they can intimidate you to do poorly – it will open a slot for them. I was pleasant to my group but didn't get chummy with them.

7) Phase II folks don't bite! As Dr. Phil says, they can't kill you - and even if they do - they can't eat you!

HAVE FUN!

"When you have completed 95 percent of your journey, you are only halfway there." ~ Japanese Proverb

❧ 4 ❧

Training Daze
FBI Academy - Quantico, VA

"If you think you can, you can. And if you think you can't you're right." ~ *Mary Kay Ash*

❧❧❧❧❧❧

I knew the sixteen (16) weeks at the FBI Academy in Quantico, Virginia would be a blur. I was nervous and excited and I had been thinking about the advice given by several agents:

1) Be physically fit <u>before</u> you get to Quantico
2) Cooperate and graduate
3) Stay in the middle of the pack

Driving through the forest to the FBI Academy was amazing. There's that certain time of day when tree shadows fall across a road that makes driving in and out of them feel like you're with paparazzi. Each opening allows a flash of brightness followed by an instant shadow. It's repeated over and over and is mesmerizing. I love that time of day. It reminds me of the warmth I always felt driving the road to my grandmother's house in Zwolle, Louisiana. Of course, one big difference was that I never heard sniper gunshots on the way to Mammaw's.

On this beautiful day, March 2, 1997, I had a lot of time to think and pray. Before I made that final turn into the FBI Academy, I slowed to a stop, took a deep breath and asked God to be with me as my life changed forever. There are not too many moments like that in life . . . reaching a cross-path with the full knowledge that the step you are about to make will take you in a completely new direction.

I made my way through the guard gate, telling them who I was and that I was reporting for new agent training. There were almost 50 people in my class so they heard that announcement many times that day. As I parked my car, I remembered the three things my mother told me:

1) Don't date while in training (she knows my weakness for attractive men)
2) Don't loan your car to anyone (she knows my soft heart for helping people)
3) Don't "counsel" and listen to people whine (again, she knows my soft heart for helping people)

Those words of wisdom would help me on many occasions during my time at Quantico, and after all . . . Mother knows best!

DORMS

I got settled in my assigned dorm with my roommate, Sandy, from New York. She was spunky, fun and her accent cracked me up. I broke out my New York accent and we had fun bantering back and forth.

Several of the dorms are set up as two suites with a connecting bathroom. There are two to a suite and the bathroom has two sinks, a shower and toilet stall (very bare). I thought this might make up for my spoiled luxury in living at home and in an apartment when I went through college. This was definitely the "dorm life" I missed.

We found out at dinner that some folks got the "cushy" dorm. These private room suites are normally given to agents coming back to Quantico for "In-Service" training. They have private bathrooms . . . with bathtubs! After the first week and total body soreness, I offered a guy $1,000 if I could use his tub. We had a good laugh about that - but he did give me his extra long sheet set to fit my single bed. They didn't tell us that normal sheets won't fit - and they don't provide a fitted sheet - just two flat sheets. It doesn't take long to learn to iden-tify quirks - one of mine is that I like the bottom sheet tight on my bed.

My area felt more like home with pictures, a comforter and the col-orful collage Natalie made for me - full of fun and encouraging messages. As I received cards throughout the training, I posted them so I was surrounded with warm, loving thoughts. Several class-mates often came by for a break from their cold white dorm rooms.

STRESS

Stress does amazing things to the body and our class counselors and supervisor told about some things to watch for . . . upset stomach, difficulty sleeping, change in appetite, etc. Well, it hit Sandy the most and she gave daily updates on whether or not she could "go." I know - TMI - it was for me too.

The Drug Enforcement Administration (DEA) also trained at Quantico while I was there. Those guys (and a very few women) were maniacs. We heard them daily at 6:00 a.m. running the stairwells.

Because of a hiring freeze, it took Sandy almost five years from the time she applied to the FBI to make it to the Academy. She finally applied to DEA as well and received an offer from DEA the same week she got the offer from the FBI. Now, seeing the training DEA was put through, she was very glad she accepted the FBI offer. There's a saying, "FBI talks, DEA kicks butt." I think you could tell those guys to go eat tree bark and they would. I met quite a few during my training and they were nice enough . . . but definitely not the sharpest tools in the shed.

We were fed piles and piles of s...s...s...sunshine and Bluff-N-Stuff (BS). As I said earlier, we were told that we were among the top 2% of the population and it was harder to get into the FBI than it is to get into Harvard. We were also told that the seat we held was coveted by hundreds of thousands of applicants. Here's a hint for the FBI Academy - most of the people that make it to Quantico definitely do NOT need their egos stroked. In fact, they would do well to explain the great responsibility new agents are taking on and the difference between a healthy self-confidence and an overbearing arrogance.

INSTRUCTORS

Most of the FBI instructors were amazing and had FBI field experience so they could teach by the book as well as give us interesting, real-life examples. Most were personable and professional with a self-assured confidence. However, a few fell short. For example, our White Collar Crime instructor was arrogant, obnoxious and condescending.

The Academy is an extremely structured environment. We were given our schedules for only one week at a time (more would've been overwhelming) and were told when and where to be practically every hour of the day. Many of the new agents despised the regimen and didn't want anyone "telling" them what to do. Unfortunately, those folks were miserable for the entire sixteen weeks of training and complained through each and every step. Others of us quickly learned to adapt and make the best of the environment. If the whiners had stepped far enough away to see the overall picture, they would realize there was logic to the scheduling and would recognize where pressure was added to measure performance in high stress environments.

Later in my career I did an informal survey of my own. I found that those who enjoyed the Academy were the SAs that followed FBI procedures in the field and learned how to do their job. The SAs that "hated" the Academy (and there were very few that fell to middle ground), were the SAs that felt they were invincible and given the keys to the kingdom when they got their badge and gun. These were very often the SAs that did what they wanted, when they wanted and broke FBI procedure any time they could. I called them the "bad guy" SAs.

FINDING WEAKNESS

One thing I learned at the Academy is that everyone has a weakness. You don't get into the FBI Academy unless you have proven ability and accomplishments. What I found was that each of us had to find our weakness and overcome it. For me, it was running.

Sandy was an amazing athlete. She had run the eco-challenge, been in a fitness magazine and she even won the weight-lifting competition at the FBI Academy. She was a short little thing, and I don't think she had an ounce of body fat on her - and she was a machine when it came to fitness training . . . and running. On our first Physical Training (PT) test, she was just shy of a perfect score and by the second test, she made the perfect score. To give you an idea of what an amazing accomplishment that is, agents that reach that level have their name engraved on a plaque at the Academy and there aren't too many names up there. Sandy was one of the confident and competent SAs. She was not egotistical and she had a great personality.

Even in her athletic excellence, Sandy had an area of some weakness - academics. I didn't have a problem with the book stuff, but I still needed help with push-ups and running. There were many nights that I would quiz Sandy to prepare for tests, and I'd be doing push-ups with her looking over her book saying, "get lower . . . break the plane" meaning the horizontal plane of your arms to the ground. She also helped me learn how to breathe properly to improve my run time.

Some SAs, especially the women, had difficulty with firearms. I was on a rifle team in my younger days and had carried a gun for 14 years so I knew how to shoot. At the beginning, I did very well on the firearms range and was told I was the best female they had. The instructors said I was on track for "Top Gun" (the best shooter in each class) and often referred to me as "Hot Shot." Knowing how to breathe while pulling the trigger was a big help. Also, I had a brother growing up and he had scared me on more than one occasion. I say that because it was very obvious to me that the female scores dropped once the targets were "faced."

The shooting targets were mounted on metal frames in front of the berm – the dirt mountain bullets lodge in behind the targets. When we first started shooting with no time limit or scores, the targets were static facing each shooter. Many did well at this stage. However, after only a few days, the targets were turned away from the shooters (where you only see the edge) and then were "faced" when our time started for each scored shooting course. When that happens, all the targets turn and lock in place with a loud bang - and scores drop.

If you hide behind a door and lunge out at a man, he may be startled but his reaction is much less than that of a woman. Most women will scream or physically jump. That same reaction was apparent when the targets "faced" with the loud bang. I suggested to the instructors that for future classes, the "facing" be made part of the practice sessions so people could get accustomed to the "facing" without their scores being affected during timed shooting courses.

We had "red-handle" guns in the dorms, painted and completely disabled that allow for practice away from the range. I worked with several women to help overcome this "startle" reflex. One exercise is to place a penny on the gun sight and keep it balanced as the trigger is pulled. Another exercise is to slightly hit the shooters gun when they pull the trigger to simulate the recoil. It's also important to keep your eyes open! It's natural to blink when a gun is fired. It's not natural (and you won't hit the target) if you close your eyes just before you pull the trigger. I got tickled that a couple of women actually closed their eyes and made a grimacing face just before they pulled the trigger, even while practicing.

After a short time, I started having difficulty with my gun jamming. Anytime a round gets jammed in the gun chamber, the protocol is to tap the weapon to dislodge rounds, pull back the slide to clear the rounds and get ready to shoot again . . . tap, rack, ready - it shouldn't happen often but we were trained how to handle it.

Soon every firearms session was an exercise in clearing my weapon and my class-mates deemed me the "Tap, Rack, Ready Queen" - not a title I wanted. After on-going problems I asked the instructors for help. They watched me shoot and shot the gun themselves. Four of them said I was doing everything right. The problem was a defective gun so they requested it be replaced.

Rather than the Academy issuing me a new gun, they continued to "rebuild" it while I watched my scores go from 98 to below 70. There was no way I could complete the courses in the time allotted when I spent so much time clearing the gun. I continued to score 100 with the shotgun and semi-automatic machine pistol but with the difficulties in clearing my sidearm, I saw the "Top Gun" award slip from my reach. One consolation was that Sandy and I were asked to be on the firearms line in an FBI recruiting video.

See a video at www.fbi.gov/hq/td/academy/sat/sat.htm

When I arrived at my first duty station, I wrote a memo to the FBI Firearms Unit Chief documenting the problems (throughout training) with a defective gun and outlining my concerns should I be involved in a shooting incident. Only then (by documenting liability) did the FBI replace the gun . . . after months of unnecessary frustration.

There were a lot of us that needed help to increase our run times. However, one man was so tall and big that he literally passed out when he ran. His body didn't get enough oxygen to feed his brain so he constantly came away from runs with scrapes on his body from falling. He was lucky he never broke his nose.

I injured my knee in the first few weeks of training which made for a very long and painful healing process. The doctor's answer was to inject cortisone, take a two week break from running and then get back to it. The nursing and physical therapy staff at the Academy is phenomenal. They helped me to heal as quickly as possible with ice, massage, stretching and Motrin, affectionately called Academy M&M's because so many people took them for pain from training injuries. My injury was minor compared to those that suffered from dislocated and shattered knees, pulled hamstrings and sprained or broken ankles. I was told that up to 80% of agents leave the Academy injured.

I had to forgo the running for the second PT test but with the encouragement and support of our class supervisor and the PT instructor (who we warmly referred to as Mr. Maniac) - I was able to pass. For those folks in training that could not heal and take the final PT test, they were . . . Recycled! That horrible word - meaning that you'd either be dropped back to graduate with a different class or you would be sent back to your processing field office until your injury healed and then return to the Academy.

It doesn't sound like a bad thing from the outside and there's not a place on the badge or credentials that gets stamped "Recycled" but inside the Academy - - - Recycle was a four-letter word. It was taboo and people did some amazing things to avoid it . . . including me. I've often wondered where that came from. If SAs are moving through the Academy sixteen weeks at a time, where does that Institutional stigma originate. I have to think that the instructors may perpetuate some of that mindset. In hindsight, the best thing I could have done was to be recycled and get back to running when I was completely healed. I continued training (in pain) and ran on an injury. I bought into the "tough guy" mentality and just kept going. The question remains if I was recycled, could I have avoided Albuquerque (my first office) altogether and been assigned elsewhere? I don't question that I could've avoided over a year of physical therapy on my damaged knee. Of course, you can't go back and "what if" your life. I believe God put me where He wanted me and provided the grace I needed.

As you may recall, Christopher Reeve had a horse riding accident and was paralyzed in 1995. My brother had been working with a group that developed a new and innovative product for the disabled and he told me about the meetings he had with the Reeve family. Also, **Somewhere In Time** is my favorite romantic movie and I had followed Christopher closely. It's interesting that one of his personal quotes was, "A hero is an ordinary individual who finds the strength to persevere and endure in spite of overwhelming obstacles." When I was running and hurting the most thinking I just couldn't go one more step, I'd remember Christopher. I was humbled and grateful that my legs were working. What he wouldn't give to feel anything in his legs again. Those thoughts and continual prayer inspired me to keep going and persevere through the pain.

I did find it interesting that they told me I HAD to pass the final PT test. I was told if I failed the run, I would not graduate - ever. That's a lot of pressure, which I used for motivation and I passed. When I got to Albuquerque, I met a male SA that never passed the final PT test due to an injury. I have no idea if his exception was made through the "Boys Club" or through other connections.

Some SAs had difficulty with tactical driving, defensive tactics, planning arrests, etc. My biggest surprise was two individuals that almost didn't make it through because they wouldn't jump off the high diving board into the pool. The exercise was to wear old pants, jump off the high dive and then tie knots in the legs and fill the pants with air (for survival floating). As a former life-guard, I didn't understand a fear of water but I definitely understood a fear of heights.

FEAR OF HEIGHTS

I went skydiving in 1991 thinking it might help get me over my fear of heights. Now I'm not afraid to jump out of an airplane but I'm still afraid to get on a roof.

Skydiving was amazing. I didn't want to go through a long "jump school" so I decided to go tandem with an instructor. My choices were 1) Crazy Eddie, I don't even want to know how he got his name, and 2) Miles Hillis, with a great reputation for doing safety checks for the surrounding area jumps. Guess who I went with? Miles was a very personable man and asked a friend to film my adventure. I'm glad to have a record of that wild day.

Miles did a very short pre-jump briefing and we were off to the wild blue yonder. Several of my friends came with me. I'm not sure

37

if it was to encourage me not to chicken out or to witness my demise - but it was an awesome experience. I told Miles I wanted to have the best experience possible because if I survived, I wasn't doing this again. We did a back flip out of the plane and then free fell for 26 seconds. My job was to pull the rip chord at 5,000 feet. Well, Miles pulled the chord at 4,500 and saved our lives. I have a tendency to say the "*" word when I go on roller coasters or exciting rides. The video proved that I screamed during the free fall . . . but with the sensory overload, I couldn't even think of a word . . . much less the "*" word so I just kept saying, "oh, oh, oh, oh, oh, oh." Now I know why you need experience with static lines (that pull the rip chord as you exit the plane) before you ever skydive on your own. There is an initial rush with the jump when you feel like you lose your stomach, but once you reach a certain velocity, you don't get that sensation any more . . . but you're still falling . . . fast! We dropped 5,500 feet in 26 seconds. We would've hit the ground in less than a minute. That's not a lot of time to think, or to forget to pull the rip chord . . . duh!

Once the parachute opened, the ride down was gentle, calm and beautiful. Miles had already briefed me on the landing. We'd flare the chute (pull down hard on two side lines) to give a little lift and then just step out on the landing. It wouldn't be more of a jolt than jumping off three steps. Yeah . . . whatever! My legs were like Jell-O pudding pops so when we landed, the "step out of it" was me awkwardly falling on him while nervously laughing. The camera man came over and gave me a kiss on the cheek and I've lived to tell the tale.

Weeks earlier, I told my parents I was thinking about taking this adventure and my dad's friend, a former Marine, assured me that I would break a leg or an arm and it was too dangerous. I tried to explain the new parachutes and how they have ways to control and steer the jump, as well as the landing speed. He came from the white cover drop military days so of course, he knew it all.

The day I got home from the jump, my mother called and asked me what I'd been "up to." She was quite surprised when I told her, "Oh, about 10,000 feet." It was (and is) fun to watch the video with family and friends.

So, back to the pool at the FBI Academy . . . two people (one male and one female) had to be coaxed to jump. It was temping to just push them in and in fact, they asked if someone could push them, but they had to do it on their own. They were told they would not graduate until they made that jump. It took about ten minutes before they worked up the courage and made the jump. When the woman hit the water, she got to the side so quickly that she swam out of her pants. I think that's when I really realized that everyone, every single person on this planet, has a weakness and/or a fear . . . of something.

TEVOC

The Tactical Emergency Vehicle Operations Center (TEVOC) training was absolutely crazy. I had a speeding ticket in my past and had gone through Defensive Driving where it was further emphasized to obey the speed limits, make gradual lane changes and not make sudden moves that might alarm other drivers.

At the FBI Academy, I was taught to drive like an absolute maniac. I knew something was up when I was given a helmet, strapped into a car with a racing body harness and told about the car's safety features which included roll bars.

My instructor was gorgeous and I admit I had a little crush on him - of course I could get in line with every other woman within 50 miles. He had a dazzling smile, a quick wit and a gentle and confident way about him that helped me to concentrate and do well. We were scored on serpentine courses, lane change exercises and various high speed driving courses.

We were also told we had to go through a backward driving test. Now keep in mind that I had trouble backing out of my driveway when I got there. But, with the right training and confidence that was placed in me, I did a great job and scored among the top in the class.

I also did very well in the skid car - a machine contraption that makes a car look like a crab with wheels. The instructor is in the passenger seat with controls to simulate driving under various conditions; hydroplane, ice, gravel, mud, etc. We were shown the "old" way of skid/spin out training where cars were heaved down a runway slicked with oil and students slammed on the brakes. Many years (and crashed cars later) the skid car was developed to allow training under adverse conditions while still giving the instructors the ability to immediately control the car by using a remote control gadget to stop all skid simulations.

Well, my dad taught me to drive on ice by doing donuts in a Kansas school parking lot. My instructor made the car as "sloppy" as possible with the controls and I still kept it under control. He was quite impressed and a bit aggravated that he couldn't make me skid out but we had lots of other people to watch for entertainment.

GORE WEEK

Early in the training, we went through what we affectionately called "Gore Week." We had lectures with many graphic and disturbing videos. This was being pushed into the deep end . . . of death. They made sure to strip away the glamour of the SA job, if only for a short time, and provide a reality check that FBI agents carry guns for a living and that means there is danger that can lead to death. It's not like the movies where a bad guy gets shot and just falls down. Even with a "fatal" gun shot, a bad guy can get off a number of rounds (bullets) before finally "bleeding out" - passing out and dying.

These lectures and videos prompted a lot of great discussions among class members and we all had to do some serious soul searching about the moral dilemma of killing another human being. I had a very clear understanding of this in my own mind. First, whatever happened to me would have to go through God. Second, if I ever had to kill a bad guy, it would be his decision. I would do what was right and attempt to handle the situation through communication. However, if the bad guy failed to follow instruction and put myself, other agents/officers, or civilians in danger he would make the decision to be shot for the safety of innocent people. It was not difficult to reconcile once I realized it's really the bad guy that makes the decision whether shots are fired.

I was told that many classes have people drop out after Gore Week. Maybe they hadn't seriously considered the gravity (or danger) of the job. I know of one person that really didn't think he'd have to carry a gun. Another one was dismissed when he was overheard in the locker room saying that he would never use his gun, no matter what. He was only going to be an agent for a year or two to boost his resume. I was thankful they left when they did. I wouldn't want those people put in a position where other lives were in danger because of their hesitancy.

We learned the FBI's Deadly Force policy. We don't shoot to kill; we shoot to stop the threat - even if it means emptying a magazine into a bad guy (13 rounds) and then reloading to keep firing. There are no warning shots or disabling shots (like shooting 'em in the knee), we shoot center mass. That, coupled with the fact that our SWAT (Special Weapons and Tactics) teams don't use rubber bullets or bean bags like some police departments, I highly advise all you bad guys to do as you're told when you encounter FBI Special Agents. With the right aftermath legal verbiage, agents can lawfully shoot you in the back.

ACTION/REACTION

This area of instruction struck me more than any others. One exercise is to take out a dollar bill and hold it on one end, perpendicular to the ground. Ask someone to put their thumb and forefinger over the center of the bill and you'll let go. If they can catch it between their fingers, they can have it. Action is always faster than reaction. Let the bill drop and you will find that they will never be able to catch it . . . even being that close. By the time their brain realizes that the bill is moving and signals the fingers to close, the bill has passed through. This is a lot of fun to do with kids.

Another exercise is to have someone hold a quarter in their hand, palm extended upward. All you do is grab the quarter before they close their hand. You can make a lot of money this way. Again, action is always faster than reaction. The application for us is that a bad guy has the advantage when the FBI is reacting to them. It is always best to be in the action position. You may have heard of "suicide by cop." Unfortunately there are people that may hold a gun to their own head threatening suicide. Knowing that action is faster than reaction, meaning the bad guy could lower that gun and fire on law enforcement or innocent bystanders, police are forced to stop the threat and shoot.

It's sobering to know that a bad guy with a knife at about 20 feet could lunge toward you and stab you before you could draw a gun and fire. Being on the reactive side of any situation is always the position of disadvantage . . . and unfortunately, reacting is most often the law enforcement side.

SPECIAL AGENTS ARE COOL

I'll never forget the first time it hit me - how cool being an FBI SA was. With the last name of Baldwin, I was #2 alphabetically for everything, placing me second on the firearms line. As I looked down the line, I saw over 40 agents - khaki pants, blue shirts, blue hats with eye and ear protection standing "at ease." It gave me chills and I felt a pride and sense of belonging. I enjoyed that moment so much that I made it a point take notice of our class uniformity.

When we first started shooting, it was March and in the Washington/Virginia area that means cold. We were all bundled up wearing sweatshirts, coats and neck scarves looking like a bunch of Michelin Men. When it snowed one day I looked to my left and saw this big, tough guy holding a sub-machine pistol - catching snowflakes on his tongue. Cool quickly turned to comical.

I also learned that being "cool" and having a personality don't necessarily go hand in hand. I suppose most folks have a tough time being cool and laughing at the same time. We had a lecture about survival where we were made to understand that even (and especially) if you get injured you don't stop fighting. You never stop fighting until you're dead. This was a very sobering lecture and it was reinforced by showing reenactments of the 1986 FBI Miami Firefight where approximately one hundred forty five (145) shots were fired (www.foia.fbi.gov/foiaindex/shooting.htm). There were two subjects killed, two SAs killed and five SAs injured. That event was a tragedy but it did force the issue to provide each agent a semi-automatic sidearm (rather than a revolver) and provide adequate protective body armor. It also reiterated the magnitude of safety and preparedness.

After in-depth discussions about survival - the instructor showed us one last video. It was Arthur's encounter with the Black Knight from *Monty Python & The Holy Grail*. I can't recommend the movie but the scene we were shown was most appropriate and is provided below:
www.angelfire.com/ny5/mpholygrail/script.html.

<>&<>&<>&<>&<>&<>&<>&<>&<>&<>&<>&<>&<>&<>

ARTHUR draws his sword and approaches the BLACK KNIGHT. A furious fight now starts lasting about fifteen seconds at which point ARTHUR delivers a mighty blow which completely severs the BLACK KNIGHT's left arm at the shoulder. ARTHUR steps back triumphantly.

ARTHUR: Now stand aside worthy adversary.

BLACK KNIGHT: (Glancing at his shoulder) 'Tis but a scratch.

ARTHUR: A scratch? Your arm's off.

BLACK KNIGHT: No, it isn't.

ARTHUR: (Pointing to the arm on ground) Well, what's that then?

BLACK KNIGHT: I've had worse.

ARTHUR: You're a liar.

BLACK KNIGHT: Come on you pansy!

Another ten seconds of furious fighting till ARTHUR chops the BLACK KNIGHT's other arm off, also at the shoulder. The arm plus sword, lies on the ground.

ARTHUR: Victory is mine (sinking to his knees) I thank thee O Lord that in thy . . .

BLACK KNIGHT: Come on then.

ARTHUR: What?

He kicks ARTHUR hard on the side of the helmet. ARTHUR gets up still holding his sword. The BLACK KNIGHT comes after him kicking.

ARTHUR: You are indeed brave Sir Knight, but the fight is mine.

BLACK KNIGHT: Had enough?

ARTHUR: You stupid *******. You haven't got any arms left.

BLACK KNIGHT: Course I have.

ARTHUR: Look!

BLACK KNIGHT: What! Just a flesh wound (kicks ARTHUR)

ARTHUR: Stop that.

BLACK KNIGHT: (kicking him) Had enough . . . ?

ARTHUR: I'll have your leg. (He is kicked). Right!

The BLACK KNIGHT kicks him again and ARTHUR chops his leg off. The BLACK KNIGHT keeps his balance with difficulty.

BLACK KNIGHT: I'll do you for that.

ARTHUR: You'll what . . . ?

BLACK KNIGHT: Come Here.

ARTHUR: What are you going to do . . . bleed on me?

BLACK KNIGHT: I'm invincible!

ARTHUR: You're a looney.

BLACK KNIGHT: The BLACK KNIGHT always triumphs. Have at you!

(editorial)

ARTHUR takes his last leg off. The BLACK KNIGHT's body lands upright.

BLACK KNIGHT: All right, we'll call it a draw.

ARTHUR: Come, Patsy. ARTHUR and PATSY start to cross the bridge.

BLACK KNIGHT: Running away eh? You yellow *******, Come back here and take what's coming to you. I'll bite your legs off!

◇◇◇◇◇◇◇◇◇◇◇◇◇◇◇◇◇◇◇◇◇

I almost fell out of my chair laughing when I saw that scene and it makes me laugh even now. However, I was pretty much laughing alone in our survival class. There were agents that actually thought the instructor was using that footage for educational purposes. I later talked to the instructor and he said showing that video was a good gauge of who in the class really "got it." There's a time to be serious and there's also a time to lighten up and laugh.

DEFENSIVE TACTICS (DT)

Special Agents have to know how to protect themselves, or so "they" say. There are some of "them" that will also tell you not to worry too much about it, just back up and shoot. We learned both techniques.

I did very well with the ground fighting and enjoyed learning the fail-safe carotid take down. The only hitch being when you use it the bad guy has to be checked out by medical personnel.

Ken was my DT partner and as a former Baltimore Police Officer, he made sure I knew how to take a guy down. I'd had some experience wrestling my brother and Ken complimented me that I wasn't "girlie" - I was "tough." I had the bruises to prove it and several times you could see Ken's hand print bruised on my arms for days. I appreciated his approach so I wouldn't have surprises in the field. I think it's a mistake for people to "train nice." They may be trying to help their partner by just going through the motions, but it doesn't do them any favors when they have to defend themselves. It's like letting someone cheat on a test. It may get you through the test, but they still don't know the material.

However, it wasn't appreciated when the Rambo guys did aggressive moves designed to break limbs in actual combat and cranked them up so much they injured their classmates in training. These Neanderthals didn't follow instruction when they were told to do the moves at "half speed." One of these over zealous guys popped my shoulder by jamming my arm too far behind my back. It took about two weeks before that pain subsided.

Ken cracked me up when we were doing weapon retention training. He backed away from the bad guy shouting "Bang, bang - don't move." Throughout the training, we laughed about his "command dyslexia" - you're not supposed to shoot first!

I also learned that I am *not* a boxer. I think they incorporate boxing into the training to make sure we all know how to be hit in the face and head. Well, boxing just kicked my butt. I already knew I could take a punch and throw one . . . I just can't always do the boxing "parry" (getting out of the way of a punch) in a graceful manner. The deflection techniques they taught just never sunk in. I did much better with simple instructions like, "don't get hit." One of the instructors had been a boxing coach at an elite university and I finally told him I was going to start charging an admission fee for his entertainment if he didn't stop laughing at me. I learned to laugh at myself too . . . and get the bad guy on the ground as soon as possible.

PRACTICAL APPLICATIONS UNIT (PAU)

An amazing part of the FBI Academy is Hogan's Alley. This is a mock town built to give us hands on operational experience during training. There's a grocery store, movie theatre, trailer park, car dealership, pool hall, hotel, apartment building, bank - pretty much everything you'd find in a real town. Most of the stores are only facades, with the insides used for storage, etc. but some are built-out for training. Actors are hired to play bad guys and give us grief . . . and lots of it.

The Bank of Hogan is robbed every other Tuesday (depending on new agent training schedules), complete with a bad guy shoot out and a bystander being shot. The class "Command Post" is notified and we head over (with FBI cars, radios, etc.) to do the investigation. The actors are great. They cry, scream, get hysterical and can't remember anything or just, "don't know . . . it happened so fast." It's just like real-life.

My assignment the day our class responded was to dust for fingerprints. All well and good, except in the field the FBI never dusts for fingerprints, that's done by local police, if done at all.

After all the investigation is complete, a mock trial is conducted with actual attorneys that come in and question us on the witness stand. I remember being asked how long a fingerprint can remain on a surface. The answer is . . . indefinitely under the right environmental conditions. However, since one of the instructors told me "about ten years," that's the answer I gave. I was quite embarrassed that the attorney knew the right answer and I didn't. That was also the moment I made note to look up the "real" answers rather than taking someone's word. I would soon learn that there are a lot of folks in the FBI that don't know the right answers so they make up what sounds good at the time to get them off the spot.

Perhaps you know folks like this. Rather than just say, "I don't know," SAs (and **lots** of supervisors) will literally make up an answer to try and look cool. That may be fine if you ask how "Dippin' Dots" are made, it doesn't work when you're working an FBI case where legal issues are at stake. By the way, Dippin' Dots are made by flash freezing ice cream mix in liquid nitrogen – www.dippindots.com.

I'd like to pass on a tip I learned during training and in the field . . . don't use a bank on Friday. Early morning may be okay but definitely not afternoon. Follow the reasoning here - bad guys are usually awake getting in trouble until the wee hours of the morning so they sleep until the late morning, early afternoon. The "weekend" starts on Friday night so the bad guys figure they don't have enough drugs to get through the party. They can't impress their girlfriends if they don't have drugs and money so they decide to rob a bank to get the money - on Friday afternoons. It's also interesting that most bank robbers only get about $1,500 and are caught rather quickly - at times in a very humorous way. Example: Bad Guy robs bank. If he's not covered in blue ink from a dye pack, he gives money to Girlfriend. Bad Guy and Girlfriend party Friday and Saturday night - end up fighting and break up. Girlfriend watches news and calls Crime Stopper Tip Line to turn in Bad Guy. Girlfriend gets Crime Stopper reward money. Girlfriend gets more spending money while the Bad Guy gets none of the money he stole plus ends up in a federal prison for over fifteen years. Those Girlfriends are running quite a racket.

The Hogan's Alley bad guys do a great job at giving us a hard time. They talk back, run and fight - anything they can think of to create chaos. It's a good preparation for worst case scenario and thankfully I never had an actual arrest where the subject(s) were even remotely close to how difficult the men and women were at Hogan's Alley.

One interesting case at Hogan's Alley involved a huge bad guy. It took five of us to get him on the ground and he was so large that he couldn't put his hands behind his back to be handcuffed. It doesn't take long to get resourceful in those situations. We strung all our handcuffs together on him . . . it looked like he was part of a chain gang.

I was the team leader for a scenario with a barricaded subject, possibly with hostages. I used the car loud speaker and talked to him . . . it seemed like forever. I gave him every positive way to end the situation, even talking about how his mother must feel knowing her son was so unhappy and in danger. The bad guy came out with his hands up and the situation ended without incident. The actor later told me he had never before come out without shots fired but I gave him good, sound reasons to end the situation peacefully so he gave up.

I had a lot of situations like that, where the trained bad guy actors were intent on shooting or being aggressive but I was able to resolve the situation without incident, and without anyone being injured. The instructors often complimented me on my ability to stay calm in dangerous and tense situations. I was also able to get confessions from the majority of subjects I interviewed but I learned that I could've gotten more information more quickly if I had kept a greater degree of discomfort with the subject. Sandy, from a sales background and I, from a Public Relations background, both had to guard against the tendency to make others feel too comfortable. We had to learn the subtle differences between building rapport and positioning to move to interrogation, which is never "comfortable."

As time went on, the exercises got more involved and difficult . . . and we added paint guns. Now, I had seen videos about paint gun games where a big splotch appeared when someone got shot. However, this is the FBI and they have their own way of doing things. They use pellets of colored soap that are the same size as bullets. The paint guns look like real guns (with certain modified identifiers). All this to say, when you get hit with a paint gun pellet, it hurts and it leaves a raised mark/bruise on your skin.

They had all kinds of exercises for us to do, each with a higher degree of difficulty. This was phenomenal training and helped all the agents in ways not possible by any other means. The instructors debriefed each operation to let us know what was done well and how it could be done better in the future . . . and we were able to repeatedly practice with various scenarios to enforce the lessons learned.

I outsmarted myself in one operation. I was tasked to be the "hostage" in the car with a bad guy actor. I suggested that I be his "girlfriend" (a bad girl) with the hostage being held at an undisclosed location. The instructors liked the twist and we went into action. As the operation unfolded, numerous FBI cars surrounded our vehicle. I started screaming, "He's going to kill me, help!" Agents screamed at me, "Get out and run." I ran behind a group of agents and while their focus was still on the bad guy car, I pulled out my "bad girl" gun from my waistband and started shooting. I shot about six of them before I saw the others turn toward me. It was like a slow motion action movie and I found myself covered in a barrage of gunfire. It was a great lesson for all of us to handcuff everyone on scene and sort out who they are after the crisis. For me, it was a great lesson not to be a bad girl anymore. My clothes were covered in orange soap and my body was marked for days.

I was also given the one class assignment to work as an Under Cover Agent (UCA). In this scenario, I would play the girlfriend of Doug, a known drug dealer working with the FBI. In guarding the identity of people that work with the FBI, there are times when an agent needs to be introduced into an operation so the SA can testify in court and protect the "snitch." A great movie about UCA operations is *Donnie Brasco*. It came out in 1997 and our class saw it together at the beginning of training. It was exciting to be watching a movie about FBI agents while we were in training to become FBI agents.

Three of the instructors were giving each other that "knowing" look and kept saying, "Oh yeah, Tracy's gonna have fun today." I didn't know if they planned for me to get shot, be held hostage or what. They made me very nervous but once we got started, I was fine.

Doug wore a body recorder and I wore a small transmitter that was monitored by the surveillance and arrest team. I would not have a weapon and I was instructed to select a "panic/safety word." This would be used if things got heated and I needed help. Once the panic word was used, back-up and the arrest team would be there immediately.

"Code Red" was the universal panic/stop/release word throughout training with DT and Practical Applications. The role players were very convincing and this ensured that everyone would be safe and have a way to stop the action if things got too intense. We also "tapped out" when we were doing different defensive holds. That means we'd tap our hand on the mat or someone's arm/leg if things got to the point of pain. Ken was always kidding around and when I would tap out, he would maintain the hold just at the point of pain and keep asking, "Are you tapping? Are you tapping?" We worked well together and he certainly kept things fun. When I underwent physical therapy later, I found myself "tapping out" when things hurt. I think the doctors and therapists wondered if I was a wrestler.

Doug and I had some time to come up with a story of how we met, where I worked, etc. We would be holding hands and getting cozy so I asked him to hold just my little finger if he felt things were getting dangerous and I needed to be on my toes. Our task was to go see Doug's drug supplier at his trailer and make a drug deal.

When we got to the trailer, I met an older man and woman. We chatted for a few minutes and they asked a lot of questions. Then they wanted to go for a ride in our BMW . . . so off we went. I called out landmarks so our team could follow us by saying things like, "We could buy another Beemer right there at the XYZ car lot," and "Look sweetie, that gazebo is so romantic."

At one point an FBI surveillance car was parked where we were trying to turn in. I shouted out the window, "Hey, ******* why don't you get out of the way." When we got back to the trailer and settled in our conversation, a young woman crawled through the window with a gun in her hand. I commented on her revolver so the team would know there was a weapon present. She wanted to play Russian roulette and I told her how stupid that was and grabbed the gun away from her. Next, the bad guys wanted us to smoke a joint with them. I told them I had to go to work so I better not do that.

Then it became clear that the young girl was Doug's former girl-friend and she didn't like me. She started cursing at me and coming after me so I got in her face, pushed her away and said, "Look, you've been ****** since you got here. I don't know what your problem is but you need to chill."

We bought a kilo of "cocaine" and I said, "Man, that's a lot of **** there." That let the team know we had the drugs, and then we left. Once we rounded the corner and let the team know we were clear, sirens blasted and the team went in to make the arrest.

During the debriefing, the instructors complimented me on doing a great job. One instructor evaluating the operation, who had done UCA operations for years, commented that I'd be a great UCA and was sure I'd be doing it at some point in my career.

The role players (bad guy actors) also told me that I did a great job. They said most UCAs are so nervous they are shaking or sweating. They won't participate or get involved in the conversation and rarely say more than yes or no to the numerous questions asked. A lot of the UCAs won't go for a ride in the car so the operation ends there without the drug deal. If the UCA fails to go, the bad guys sometimes don't come back to the trailer. Although the best scenario is not to leave the location, you can't leave the FBI bad guy alone with the real bad guys.

They also said that many of the UCAs use the panic word when the girl comes in with a gun. The team swoops in and there's a shoot out. Doug said they tried to trip me up but I was relaxed and handled everything they threw at me. The young girl said that no one had ever gotten in her face before and she didn't know what to do so she just backed down.

Doug also told me that no one had ever worked out a signal for him to use with the UCA so he had a way to communicate if things were heating up. He thought that was a great idea.

NATIONAL ACADEMY (NA)

National Academy (NA) also trains at the FBI Academy. This branch of the Academy accepts only the "best of the best" in police/law enforcement from the US and other countries, a top police training academy for experienced officers if you will. The selection criterion to NA is quite rigorous and the officers have received top recognition and recommendations to be accepted. The officers were mostly older and almost exclusively men. In fact, I don't remember meeting a single female from the US going through NA, not during my time at training, nor the numerous times I returned for In-Services.

There are some really great police officers out there, but at NA, many officers I encountered (deemed the cream of the crop), were a terrible disappointment. Their behavior was deplorable. What I learned was that the "reputation" of NA is impeccable for those officers that come for training as well as those that graduate. However, once at the Academy, they treat NA like a Spring Break beach. I couldn't believe these were our top police officials . . . and I was shocked that they could stay drunk for such an extended period of time.

I had been warned to stay clear of the Academy bar, "The Boardroom" - which was little more than an open room with tables. Instructors, NA, FBI new agents in training and FBI SAs returning for In-Service training were known to "let loose." In other words, get as drunk as possible and in some cases, to literally crawl back to their dorm rooms. There was no limit to what was "accepted" because they justified that they weren't "driving" home. One of the Class Counselors repeated this behavior so often that he was ineffective in his duties (consistently hung-over) and was sent back to his field office. Most folks just made fools of themselves at night with the unspoken rule not to discuss what happened in the light of day.

I know this sounds like I'm just no fun, but I do know how to have fun and it doesn't include drinking to a stupor because it's accepted and expected. I can count on one hand the number of times I was in the Boardroom over the course of my nine year career. I didn't have the regrets of other females that were enthusiastically bought drinks to the point of losing total control and living with the events that followed. It could be in someone's shared room, the multiple laundry rooms or any number of other locations. It seems that the top of the dryers was especially popular. In fairness, I found most of the FBI instructors to be very responsible in their socializing and they handled themselves well. Also, I don't remember ever seeing a female instructor in the Boardroom.

It didn't take long to understand that the FBI Academy is a glorified name for a free-for-all fraternity house. It was also the first time I heard the FBI motto . . . what happens at the Academy, stays at the Academy. That was modified further in the field to, what happens on Temporary Duty (TDY), stays on TDY. It gives a whole new meaning to "Don't ask, don't tell."

NA had their own *drunk fest* area known as "The Grove." This is a small wooded patch of grass just outside the front entrance to the Academy scattered with a few picnic tables.

I was invited (and went) only one time. I was so disturbed by the conversations (about victims and arrogant stories about spiteful actions by police officers toward civilians) and by what I saw that I never went back. From my understanding, only one or two officers from any location will attend NA at the same time. That said, you have numerous Police Chiefs, Lieutenants, Captains, Sergeants and "outstanding" officers coming together with little, if any accountability. They brag that "anything goes" and the only rule enforced is "no cameras allowed."

Raised in an Army home, I had always respected authority to include police officers, especially high ranking officials. I know there are great ones out there but my experience at the Academy diminished my respect for police officers as a whole. When I went to The Grove, I witnessed the ongoing "butt darts" competition.

Keep in mind that alcohol, and large quantities of alcohol are major factors in this competition. The two "competitors" placed a plastic cup 3/4 filled with beer on the ground at the end of their lane. When the "referee" gave the signal, each competitor took a quarter and locked it between his butt cheeks. Each "waddled" down their lane, keeping the quarter clenched in place, turned around in the squatting position, and with the crowd cheering "take a dump," released the quarter into the beer cup. Once in the cup, the competitor picked up the cup with his mouth, drank the beer and with hands lifted in the victory position, showed the quarter lodged between his teeth. The first to finish was deemed the winner and would take on another competitor. This went on for hours until the competitors could only stagger down the lanes and fall to the ground. Very impressive for our top police officials, huh?!

I understand that law enforcement work is stressful and everyone needs to be able to let their guard down. However, I was astonished throughout my career that the only coping mechanism used seemed to be alcohol. I also believe that, especially in highly regarded positions, there's a time and place to "let loose." The behavior I witnessed is not appropriate at the highly esteemed FBI Academy. I think it sets the wrong tone for the entire law enforcement career - but Academy officials never even discouraged the behavior. In hindsight, I should've recognized it as a taste of disappointments to come.

You would think that being behind the secured walls and guard gate of the FBI Academy would offer some measure of security. I didn't always feel that way.

After the first month at the Academy, I stayed at hotels over the weekends to study and spend time with my friends. One night, returning to the Academy, I was stopped by a large group of NA officers in the dark parking lot. With plastic beer cups in hand, these men surrounded me making cat calls and inappropriate comments while they grabbed at me. They slurred and slobbered spit on me saying that they had to do a full body cavity search before I could go in the Academy. I physically pushed them off me and was able to get through them and to the lighted entrance. I have no idea how far those men would've taken their antics. My point here is that I should not have been subjected to that behavior - especially by elite police officers.

WHO AM I GOING TO BE?

A question my sister and I discussed while I was going through FBI training was "Who am I going to be when I get out of here?" I knew I needed self confidence regarding law enforcement matters and I had a lot of FBI "stuff" to learn, but I didn't want my core values to change and I certainly did not want to become arrogant and self-centered. Having a laser focus and direction in training is great but I knew this controlled environment was not "real."

We had some very talented individuals in NAC 97-10 but it didn't take long before the healthy self-confidences initially observed gave way to excessive arrogance and superior attitudes. I made the choice to separate from that "gang" for drinking outings and other activities.

Not that I didn't have a few fun nights to go out, eat dinner and sing karaoke until the wee morning hours . . . but it rarely stopped with just fun. More often, it included the guys (and sometimes women) getting sloppy drunk and groping all over each other (or strangers). Those encounters resulted in ongoing regretful sagas for days and weeks to come. It was like high school all over again. Being the designated driver got old and I stopped going . . . but not before I experienced the full glory of a staggering classmate, drunk out of his mind, playing "Camp Town Races" with his nose on a baby grand piano at the Academy. No question it was funny, but it's not the kind of "highlight" I was hoping for.

"BOY'S CLUB"
First Glance

It's amazing how the FBI can make and break any rule they want. We were all told from the beginning that if you lie - you're out . . . if you cheat - you're out. These are very simple rules and more than expected at the premier law enforcement, distinguished FBI training Academy.

The "Camp Town Races" guy was great. He was liked by everyone (including me), very personable, bright and full of potential. He'd even been a real clown with balloon animals and all. That said he liked to party . . . a lot! One weekend he did a little too much partying and didn't make it back to the Academy until the wee hours of the morning. Not a problem, except we had an assignment due and he had blown it off. However, he did manage to turn in a paper.

Our instructor was suspicious about the similarities between his paper and his roommates' paper so they were both questioned. Apparently Mr. Party helped himself to his sleeping roommates computer disk, made some minor changes to the file, printed it out and put his name on it. In the real world that's called cheating, plagiarism, dishonesty - pick the word you want – but it's wrong . . . he knew it was wrong . . . and he did it anyway. When questioned, he told the truth and had a moment of clarity to exonerate his roommate.

So here's the dilemma - rather than admit he partied too much and didn't do his assignment - risking getting a poor grade (which could mean dismissal from the Academy), he opted to cheat (a definite cause for dismissal) and he got caught. According to the rules of the FBI Academy, this was a clear case of dismissal . . . right!? Wait . . . do you remember I told you he was well liked? In fact, he even put balloon animals on the instructor's heads when they were drinking together in the Boardroom. Now what do you think? Well, they didn't dismiss him. In fact, their idea of "severe discipline" was to make him graduate two weeks behind us. Yep, he lied and got away with it. The message sent by FBI Officials was very clear . . . to Mr. Party and to the rest of us - in fact it was clear to everyone in the FBI - the FBI Rules will only be applied to those we don't like. The "Boy's Club Members" are exempt.

Another "interesting" case involved a very odd fellow I'll call Ned. When we first arrived at the Academy, we were all asked to stand up in the classroom and tell everyone why we wanted to be an FBI Special Agent. We were seated alphabetically so there was only one person before me and I was very thankful when they started in the back of the room. Most folks said their father's (or grandfathers) had been FBI agents and that's all they ever wanted to be. Some went to school with the sole intent of becoming an agent. That really put me on the spot because my experience was so very different. I had not even considered the FBI as a career option until one year ago . . . and now I was in training. There's no way to dress that up so I just told the truth (and watched mouths drop) and made sure to include that I felt honored to be there.

Ned was a completely different story. As we all came to learn (though it should never have been discussed), Ned's daddy was a high ranking FBI Official. Ned failed the entrance tests (plural – meaning he failed the written Phase I and oral interview Phase II) each . . . several times. That begs the question, "Then why is Ned here?" I was told that you can only retake each phase of testing one time (each after one year intervals) so how did Ned manage to manipulate the system after failing numerous times? I'm sure you're catching on a lot quicker than I did - "Boy's Club . . . it was daddy!" His son was obviously not FBI SA material but since daddy wanted him in – he was in. Ned didn't tell that story when he stood up. Instead, he told us that he was a very friendly guy and a good listener. He wanted to be friends with each of us. If we needed to talk or needed someone to be there, Ned was our guy. The instructor finally interrupted him so Ned would sit down but not before the rest of us rolled our eyes in concern that we had a very "different" guy on our hands.

Ned had difficulty with everything - and more alarming, he had no common sense. It was obvious that the instructors were not keen on Ned being forced on them from daddy - so although there were numerous times we all helped each other with operations - we had explicit instructions not to help Ned. That may not look "fair" at first glance, but I do think it's good to challenge people and the instructors wanted to make sure Ned's elevator was going up to the top floor. This created an opportunity for Ned to take full credit for his work and to shine in planning arrest operations. Unfortunately, Ned loaded six agents into one car to make an arrest (even a novice knows better than to put all your eggs - and agents - in one basket). He was driving the car and parked it directly in front of the bad guy's house. I think Ned watched too many bad FBI movies. Our bad guy stuck a rifle out the window and shot all the agents . . . oops!

The next big blunder I remember was on the firearms range with Ned's shotgun. I don't need to tell you that mistakes can <u>not</u> happen when guns and real bullets are involved. You don't get a second chance. If we did not have personal control of the shotgun, meaning carrying it with the barrel up and finger off the trigger, the gun was to be benched . . . meaning placing it on the ground with the barrel facing downrange (away from everyone). Ned wasn't thinking (one of the many times) and he propped his shotgun up on a shaky piece of thin wood placed in a cement slot so it would stand erect to simulate a barricade. He was in the middle of the range and all I remember was someone shouting to "get down." I wasn't sure if that meant we needed to hit the deck or it was directed to Ned to get the shotgun down . . . either way, it was a very tense moment. Had that gun fallen off balance it could've fired when it hit the ground and there's no telling what direction or who would've been hit by the stray slug. You don't normally recover from a shotgun blast. There was no question that Ned put each one of us in physical danger.

Even then, Ned was still with us. He was finally booted out just before our National Security classified briefing. I heard he was sent back to his processing office and was working as a support employee. Many years later I heard he was suing the FBI to be an agent.

I don't care who Ned's daddy is, he didn't belong in our class or any agent class. His dad knew it, the FBI knew it and based on his performance, I'm sure Ned knew it too. It's sad to me that by manipulating the system, Ned was permitted to waste a class seat where a qualified SA candidate should've been.

THE GOOD GUYS

It's often said that you can tell a lot about someone by their friends and you become like the people you associate with. Well, I made a conscious decision to be around good people - people that I'd want to be more like, not people that had questionable morals, intentions and/or character - that's a huge turn off for me. I'm not that way and I don't want to become like that so I knew I needed to guard against changing. As each week passed, more and more classmates believed they were given the keys to the kingdom and were officially "hot ****" – it was quite an amazing thing to witness.

Ken had seen this in the police department world and we talked more openly and privately about it as the weeks went by. He also noticed about half way through training that classmate conversations were developing into full gossip sessions. He didn't trust people like that and he started pulling away from the "clique." He and I, and a small group of others, spent quite a bit of time together . . . very positive time. A group of us went out to dinner for my birthday and someone made the comment that "We have such a cohesive class." One of the girls responded, "Cohesive my ***. It's like a bunch of sharks. They wait for someone to get nipped and then go in for the kill."

LEVELING & HOT DOGS

Leveling is an interesting phenomenon and one that I would not only witness, but also be subjected to in the years to come. Just as water moves to find one level . . . so do people. Let's say there is a group of people we'll call the B's. Although sometimes successful, B's are usually just getting by - the underachievers that have issues of insecurities and feelings of inadequacy. B's see others (the A's) "above" them. They are resentful and jealous that A's have surpassed them . . . in work, in doing the right thing, in social standing, in relationships, in opportunities, in happiness – it could be in any area of life. Rather than be inspired to do the work required to come up to a higher level and expect more of themselves, B's take shots at the A's to bring them down. It's the only way B's can feel better about themselves . . . to see themselves at the same level as the A's. If B's would only use some of their negative energy to find their internal integrity and do a little work, B's could become A's. Of course then they find themselves as the targets for other B's in life.

There are two kinds of frankfurters in the world - Weenies and Hot Dogs. Weenies are the people that whine and complain all the time. The cup is never half full or half empty - they gripe that they never even got a cup. Nothing ever goes their way and you don't dare ask how they are because they will take 15 minutes to corner you and describe, in detail, their measly existence . . . and why you should feel sorry for them. They are too miserable to entertain a positive thought. They also don't like anyone being anything but a Weenie and will try desperately to bring down the Hot Dogs.

Hot Dogs are go-getters. They are the people reaching for new heights. They bring wisdom to life and are sought after for advice. They always have a smile on their face and don't seem to have a care in the world. They walk with energy and their eyes are bright and inviting. They are productive and always thinking of the next way to improve a project, help someone or improve their own life. Hot Dogs have great friends and great relationships. If you hear murmuring and negativity . . . it's most likely a Weenie griping about a Hot Dog!

I became more and more low-key, watching and observing my classmates - which made me a wild woman on the weekends (wild in fun – not in alcohol). I'd meet up with my best friend, Debbie and my boyfriend, Jim and we'd shoot pool, go dancing, go on long Harley rides, to community events and parks, and we laughed a lot. It was the only time during my training that I felt I could really trust the people around me, let my guard down and be "me."

Debbie and I had been great friends since 1992 when we met at the First Baptist Church. She was like a sister to me and had such an ease and fun spirit about her. She had always been there in the good times and the bad and she was such an encouragement when things got tough.

In the FBI, they say most of our friends will be in law enforcement because there's a tendency to have an "Us vs. Them" attitude. People on the inside will understand how difficult it is and what we're going through. It may be true that insiders will understand but I think having non-law enforcement friends keeps perspective that we're not "holier than thou" and that the FBI is a job – it should not be your entire life.

As time went by at the Academy, I found myself spending more and more evenings alone. I'd study, work out, read, call my family or go to the Academy Chapel to pray and play the piano. It was a quiet, reflective and connective time with God. I was getting more and more discouraged by the arrogance that was taking over so many people as the weeks went on. I often wondered how I'd missed the "Arrogant SA 101" class, but I was determined to keep dodging it.

FBI GRADUATION

Graduation day was awesome and friends and families were invited to attend. The FBI Director (Louis Freeh at that time) gave us our credentials and there was a big ceremony with all the pomp and circumstance. My family was only with me in thought and prayer. After discussing the logic of the long trip from other states for a short two hour ceremony and lots of craziness packing up to leave . . . we decided it made a lot more sense to spend time together when I went back to pack my household goods and travel to my first duty station.

Our class supervisor was from Alabama and was very supportive and encouraging toward me. She said she'd be my surrogate family and gave me a big hug after I got my credentials. Debbie, Jim and two other friends came to support me on the big day and it couldn't have been better. Okay, it would've been great to have my entire family there but seeing that the private jet was tied up and the penthouse suites were already booked, it worked out just fine.

We all voted James to be our graduation spokesman (he lasted about three years before he resigned from the FBI). He was a former police officer and epitomized the public persona of an FBI Agent in the way he looked, walked, talked and breathed . . . the traditional FBI Poster Boy. I don't remember what he said in his commencement speech but we were all proud - and we took an oath and swore the following:

> *I will support and defend the Constitution of the United States against all enemies, foreign and domestic; that I will bear true faith and allegiance to the same; that I take this obligation freely, without any mental reservation or purpose of evasion; and that I will well and faithfully discharge the duties of the office on which I am about to enter. . . So help me God.*

Did you notice God in this? I did!

We walked across the stage and were officially welcomed into the FBI as Special Agents. I remember that as a really great day. I had given 100% in training at the FBI Academy and I felt support, encouragement and love - - - as well as pride and an amazing sense of accomplishment. I was ready to go out into the world and make a real difference.

Most of the class said their good-byes at the graduation ceremony and I was able to say special words to those I'd been close to. Actually, we'd been preparing for this day for quite a while. After I packed up to leave the Academy as a new SA, I made the rounds to see my instructors and gave them thank you notes/gifts and good-bye hugs. I also saw the firearms demonstration where they were using a shotgun to blast fruits and vegetables. Nothing like a slug through a head of lettuce to get the crowd fired up.

As I drove away, I realized that I had been on an amazing journey. I savored each moment at the FBI Academy and I learned an awful lot. I also realized that I had only touched the tip of the iceberg. I had a lot to learn and truthfully, just as a new college graduate - I didn't even know what I didn't know.

This would've been a good place to end my FBI career - on a positive note - because I had no idea how difficult and devastating the next nine years of my life would be.

ASSIGNMENTS

I worked incredibly hard throughout the FBI training and scored toward the top of the class in almost every area (the exception being PT). I got a very nice compliment from our class supervisor that I was the "FBI Special Agent Total Package. They're looking at you." I suppose "they" were the upper level personnel that would decide where to assign me for my first duty station.

There's an ongoing joke in the FBI that agents are assigned to their first office through a special and secret process . . . a monkey, at FBI Headquarters, throwing darts at a map. We each ranked the 56 FBI Field Offices in the order of preference but that didn't mean anything. Those that highly ranked New York or Los Angeles got pretty close, others got close to the bottom. In fact we all gave money toward a pot for the "loser" - the guy that got the lowest on his list . . . in our class it was around 40th.

Sandy (a native New Yorker) couldn't imagine going anywhere else and she returned to New York. I told her if I got assigned to New York - to please shoot me in the head! We heard a lot of stories about agents that requested smaller offices but were assigned to the biggest offices, New York, Los Angeles, Chicago, etc. They graduated from the Academy and never showed up, refusing to adjust to the drastic cultural (and family life) change of a big city. The FBI wasted thousands of dollars in training and the Academy graduate simply listed "Special Agent" on their resume.

I was told that DEA has a much more effective process. Each class is told what offices are available and the agents work it out among themselves as to who goes where. I suppose they use a selection order by class ranking. Whatever the method, they seemed to be more satisfied with their assignments.

I was assigned to Albuquerque, New Mexico. I didn't know much about Albuquerque, which is to say that I didn't even know how to spell it. I heard it was a desert - a "dry heat" and there was a balloon fiesta every year. Having moved throughout my life, I looked at this assignment as a new adventure and was excited and full of hope. I even created an outgoing message on my answering machine about it -

(Sung to the Oscar Meyer Bologna tune)

> My new home has a weird name . . .
> It starts with A - L - B . . .
> Then it has a U - Q - U - E - R . . .
> and ends with Q - U - E . . .
> It's hot and dry and far away . . .
> But the word is that I'm here to stay . . .
> So leave your name, I'll call you back . . .
> And we can have a real nice chat . . . [Beep]

Looking back I realize that my success through FBI training is what led to the devastating assignment of Albuquerque. The FBI could only send a strong, independent, successful woman to handle the atrocities in the Albuquerque pit and I believe they reasoned if anyone could handle it, I could. They knowingly sent me like a lamb to slaughter.

ALBUQUERQUE, NM

When I arrived at the Albuquerque FBI office, I saw signs posted stating "This Office Condones Sexual Harassment" ordered by a judge through an Equal Employment Opportunity (EEO) lawsuit won by a female SA in Albuquerque - since transferred to another office. There were only a handful of female Special Agents working in and around the FBI Albuquerque Division when I arrived. Just four and a half years later, one female SA had committed suicide, four female SAs resigned, one female SA was indicted and I was transferred to the FBI Houston office.

There were many times I thought I must have done something wrong for God to send me to such a terrible place. Was He punishing me? Was He teaching me? Had He completely forgotten about me? Those answers will not be found on this side of Heaven. What I do know is that God stretched me more than I ever thought possible (throughout my FBI experience) and I've learned to trust Him. Even though I don't understand why He allowed so many difficulties, I believe His Word that He uses <u>ALL</u> things together for my good. That means what the FBI meant for evil, God will use for my good.

❧❧❧❧❧❧❧

As for you, you thought evil against me, but God meant it for good, to bring about that many people should be kept alive, as they are this day. Genesis 50:20 (AMP)

*And we know that God causes **all things** to work together for good to those who love God, to those who are called according to His purpose. Romans 8:28 (NAS)*

MP3:
Sub-Machine Pistol

Posted Outside
FBI Gym

Handcuffing
Techniques

Hogan's Alley PAU

Teamwork!

No Pain, No Gain!?!

TEVOC - Skid Car

Paint Gun Operation

*Old Credentials
(Without Security Enhancements)*

*Hogan's Alley
Bank Robbery*

FBI SA Graduation

*Police Helicopter
Ride-a-Long*

✐ 5 ✐

Rambo FBI
&
The Downward Spiral

"Important principles may, and must, be inflexible."
~ Abraham Lincoln

✐✐✐✐✐✐

My mother traveled cross-country with me to find housing and get settled in Albuquerque. It was a great adventure and we stopped along the way to see the sights . . . like Ivy Green in Tuscumbia, Alabama - the birthplace of Helen Keller; Graceland in Memphis, Tennessee - home of Elvis Presley; a huge outdoor crucifix located in the Texas panhandle and a great visit over the July 4th holiday with my sister.

We found an apartment, received my household goods and created a home in less than a week. Then I got a call to report to the FBI office a day early (throughout my career I never heard of an agent being required to report early). My supervisor would come by and pick me up about 6:30 a.m.

Since most employees didn't get to the office until 8:00 or later, our 7:00 arrival meant a tour of the office layout and introductions to empty chairs. I met my squad-mates as they came in and my cubicle was soon buzzing with activity. It is best described as "moths to light" and several comments were made about the commotion I generated. It was certainly unlike any other "first day on the job" I ever experienced. The first time I met a support employee helping me with relocation paperwork, she complimented me as beautiful and then added with a leering tone, "Boy are the guys gonna love you!" I felt like I was a piece of meat thrown to a hungry pack of dogs.

I also found it difficult to find a church home. For years, a significant part of my life had been dedicated to serving God at Whitesburg Baptist Church in Huntsville, Alabama; Senior Pastor - Dr. Jimmy Jackson . . . who had been like a second father to me since 1987. I played clarinet in the orchestra, was a leader in the Adult Singles Department and was the Drama Director. I made meaningful lifelong friendships and we all helped each other to deepen our relationships with the Lord.

Albuquerque churches were best summarized by a pastor at Hoffmantown Church when he said they were "a mile wide and an inch deep." Rather than the focus being on God, it was on cliques, judging others and being seen. I auditioned and was accepted in the orchestra, seated second chair. The woman in first chair was unfriendly to say the least. She literally looked me up and down each week and then ignored me. When I visited the Singles Bible Study, no one even spoke to me. It didn't take long before I left the orchestra and eventually the church.

I was voted in as a member of the Albuquerque Junior League and participated for over a year. I enjoyed the philanthropic activities but many of the women were superficial and downright snobby. Others were busy with kids and family life.

Elaine was my saving grace. I met her through an ex-boyfriend and she introduced me to her Bunco group where I found genuine women that were down-to-earth, warm and fun. We got together once a month and laughed until our sides hurt. These women became my dear friends for years to come.

When family and friends asked how things were going with an excited expectancy, I often said I was just getting my feet wet and learning the job. The truth is that within the first two months of being in Albuquerque, I was shaken by what I saw going on in the FBI. By December 1997, just six months after becoming an SA, I went home for Christmas and broke down as I told my parents that the FBI was nothing more than a huge disappointment. I believed in what the FBI stood for but I was not seeing those positive ideals living within the walls of FBI Albuquerque.

I was assigned to the White Collar Crime (WCC) Squad as well as the Special Operations Module (SOM). SOM was a team of agents from numerous squads, thrown together to conduct surveillance because the FBI Albuquerque Division was not large enough to have a dedicated Special Surveillance Group (SSG). I worked these two areas for over two years. In WCC, I worked cases involved Bank Fraud, Bankruptcy Fraud, Interception of Communication, Health Care Fraud, Computer Intrusion, Securities/Commodities Fraud and Wire & Mail Fraud Schemes. SOM work primarily involved Drug and Foreign Counter-Intelligence (FCI) cases where I was repeatedly tasked as the team leader. I was later assigned to an FCI squad and worked the largest espionage case in the Bureau. I was also appointed as the Awareness of National Security Issues and Response (ANSIR) Coordinator to educate and liaison with critical infrastructure personnel throughout the city and state. FBI Headquarters slated the materials and presentation I created to be used throughout the nation.

I also coordinated the Combined Federal Campaign (CFC) and exceeded the goal by 61%, the highest amount ever; was a member of the FBI Recreation Association and the Employee Assistance Committee; was the Albuquerque Division Editor for the internal FBI national publication, *The Investigator*; and mentored a fourth grade student.

The "work" of the FBI was rarely an issue for me. I had interesting, challenging cases; I did my job well and was rated highly on my performance evaluations in spite of the appalling behavior I witnessed and the way I was treated. I also didn't have any issues with the bad guys. As ridiculous as it may sound, the bad guys treated me with more respect than the FBI ever did. It reminds me of the late Steve Irwin who said he trusted animals more than people. Animals stay true to their nature, even if that nature is to kill you - unlike people who pretend to be one thing and then swing around and knife you in the back.

There were several times I thought about quitting. However, each time I was close to making that decision I would work a case, encounter a victim or interview a witness where I was personally thanked for my dedication to the FBI and for helping them . . . and would go on to say the FBI needed more people like me. I was one of the "good guys" so why was I having so many difficulties? Because I bought into what the FBI said they are – not what they <u>actually</u> are. I also didn't know what to do. If the FBI is the "best of the best - the top 2% of the population" and it's horrendous - then where's the top? Where do you go to find the best?

I had so many awful experiences in Albuquerque that it's difficult to select a sampling to include here . . . there are literally hundreds to choose from. Unknowingly at the time, these situations were working together to create a downward spiral. By the fall of 1999, just over two years after becoming an SA, I was planning my suicide.

ON THE STREET

Although no arrest plan can fully account for unforeseen variables, a plan should be made none the less. The FBI arrests I witnessed (and found myself supporting as a participant) were off-the-cuff and had little if any consideration for agent or public safety.

♦ My first arrest was conducted within a few weeks of my arrival in Albuquerque. It was a complete fiasco. I was asked to assist in the arrest of a subject that was armed and dangerous, expected to either fight or run from law enforcement.

During new agent training, we were told that the last FBI agent killed in the line of duty was a female, new to a division, conducting an arrest operation. She did not have FBI identification visible and was shot by two FBI agents that did not know her.

> *On October 5, 1985, Special Agent Robin L. Ahrens, who was assigned to the Phoenix FBI Office, was fatally wounded while participating with other Agents in the apprehension of fugitive Kenneth Don Barrett. The fugitive was sought for unlawful flight to avoid prosecution for armed robbery. SA Ahrens was fatally shot by other Agents at the arrest scene who mistook her for an armed associate of the fugitive. SA Ahrens was the first female Special Agent to be killed in the line of duty.*
>
> *SA Ahrens was born in May of 1952 in St. Paul, Minnesota. After receiving a Bachelor of Fine Arts Degree from Utah State University in 1974, and a Media Specialist Degree from James Madison University in Virginia, she entered on duty as a Special Agent in 1984. SA Ahrens completed her training in June of 1985.*
>
> www.fbi.gov/libref/hallhonor/ahrens.htm

Considering a time period for relocation after FBI Academy graduation, SA Ahrens worked for approximately three (3) months before she was shot dead by her own "back-up."

I was extremely concerned about the Albuquerque operation I was involved with since there had been no pre-arrest briefing (a mandatory process according to training), I did not know what the subject looked like and other agents conducting this arrest did not know me. I put on my FBI protective vest and was told to take off the FBI front label so the subject would not see it when I approached the scene. I remembered something my mom told me, "Be safe, or I'll kill you myself." I refused to remove the FBI insignia, starting the first of a long line of issues where I was placed in the position to do what I knew was right (and what I was taught by the FBI in training), or succumb to Rambo FBI agents with seniority, ego and negative attitudes. Call me "Safety Girl" – but you don't get a second chance when bullets are involved. I think testosterone often interfered with male agent brain function.

The FBI car radios were not operational so the vehicle I was in (with a crusty, seasoned SA) pulled to the side of another arrest team vehicle driving at approximately 40 mph, and they yelled out the window to each other regarding set up position for the arrest *(are you kidding me)*!!!

I heard that our car would be positioned with my side toward the subject's apartment so I asked, "Should I get in the back seat behind you?" He was not concerned but said, "Sure, if you want to . . . that might be a good idea." I climbed over the seat to position myself away from the subject.

As we approached the scene, the subject was immediately spotted sitting outside his apartment and we moved in. Intimidated by the team of FBI agents with guns drawn, the man wet himself with our announcement of "FBI, don't move!" Unlike the movies, we don't say "Freeze."

While standing in the parking lot waiting to transport the subject, I met several other agents (I was the only female SA on scene). Because he looked at me just before relieving himself, I was the hot topic. If the guys (SAs) wanted to scare someone, take the chic along and the bad guys will give up. Several other comments were made toward me in jest and they made jeering comments about my protective vest. I saw that the other agents were not vested and I felt these comments were made to embarrass or belittle me for being safety conscious. Apparently the possibility of bullets and death were not an issue . . . these guys didn't think it was "cool" to wear protective vests.

This was my first arrest and my first (of many to come), realization that the FBI often places agents and civilians in physical danger. The Rambo FBI swept in, pulling guns in a densely populated apartment area. There was no attempt to plan a safer time, place or method to make this arrest and with dumb luck, it worked out alright. Numerous individuals were unnecessarily placed in danger but because no shots were fired, the guys congratulated each other on a job well done.

In training, we were told that every operation (especially arrests) consist of a briefing before (so everyone knew the plan), and a de-briefing after, to discuss what happened and ways to improve for the future. Well, that's what they say! That's not what happens!

In my nine years as an FBI SA, and the many arrests and operations in which I participated, there was not one time that FBI management, nor Case Agents, called for a de-briefing to identify what happened and ways to improve. Unfortunately, a cancer of arrogance exists among FBI SAs and management that prohibit any appearance of im-perfection. Ignorance is bliss.

◆ During New Agent training we learned the proper vehicle posi-tions and procedures to conduct felony car stop operations. This type of arrest is not optimal due to the myriad of variables and lack of sub-ject control. However, with subjects that pose an extreme danger, it may be necessary. Of particular concern during a felony car stop is getting the subject out of the vehicle and in custody. We were trained to "call out" the subject with weapons drawn and issue commands to place the subject on the ground. Only then is it safe to approach and handcuff the subject. Conducted in this manner, an arrest has a high degree of success and exposes agents to minimal danger, the focus being safety and control.

As part of the Albuquerque SOM, we were conducting a surveil-lance operation hours outside of Albuquerque. It was after 10:00 p.m. and we were in a remote desert area with absolutely no light sources. After some time, the Case Agent directed that we were to "take him down," meaning to conduct a felony car stop. I was the first vehicle behind the subject with other cars spaced over several miles. We be-gan to close the gaps between our surveillance vehicles and I called over the radio for the team leader to take lead position.

There is little chance that any of the older agents remembered (or ever knew), training scenarios. There was no direction as to who would assume each position during the stop . . . neither planning, nor safety, was considered. The lead agent engaged his lights and siren so the arrest was on. The stop was conducted like a swarm of flies. Vehicle locations put agents in crossfire positions and the lead agent jumped over the hood of his car (Starsky & Hutch style), yanked the subject out of his vehicle and threw him to the ground, putting the agent in my direct line of fire. I holstered my weapon and assumed a position to assist with the physical control of the subject.

It turns out the Case Agent had identified the wrong vehicle and we had followed it for hours. An innocent man was roughed up, cursed at and was adamantly accused of being a drug dealer. He did have a small plastic bag wrapped with duct tape in the glove compartment . . . his fishing license (duct tape keeps it afloat). There was no need for the FBI to stop this vehicle. I believe the Case Agent was getting impatient by the late hour and the long drive back to Albuquerque. Rather than follow the subject to fully identify him, or have a local police officer make a routine traffic stop to identify him, the Case Agent placed an innocent citizen in danger. This could happen to you or anyone you know.

♦ On another operation, we were set up on a residence with only limited information. We did not know how many individuals were in the residence, if any weapons were present, or if the individuals were on drugs. A call was placed to obtain additional assistance but no other resources were available at the time. The next instruction was to go in anyway. Another example of "Rambo" FBI.

♦ A felony car stop was conducted in the center lane of a six lane thoroughfare during rush hour traffic. There was no consideration what-so-ever to plan and implement a safer time and/or location. Agents swarmed the vehicle (that had blacked out windows) without even knowing how many people were in the vehicle. Agents had guns pointed directly in both the driver and passenger windows. This presented a devastating crossfire situation and put them in imminent danger if the occupants were armed and aggressive. In my opinion, countless civilians were unnecessarily placed in danger by this "Rambo" arrest.

◆ During one SOM drug operation conducted about an hour outside of Albuquerque, I was made the team leader and the drug supervisor monitoring radio traffic from the office. The subjects were "out of pocket" (lost) at one point but after a short time, a team member located their vehicle at a restaurant. I went across the highway and backed into a parking space in front of a small novelty shop. The subject came out of the restaurant, got in his vehicle, drove across the highway to the strip mall where I was parked, drove slowly by my car and returned to the restaurant.

I was concerned I had been burned (identified as law enforcement) and called out that I was "not only burned, but might be crispy" and that I was going in the shop in case they were still watching me. I went in the store and found a corner mirror I used to watch the door. The subject returned, came in the shop and spoke with familiarity to a sales associated (who may have contacted him when I arrived). Because drug cases often involve violent subjects, I was concerned that a confrontation may ensue but was confident the SOM team would arrive and provide back up assistance. I bought a candle and spoke with the sales associate telling her, "I'm Susan and I was supposed to meet my friend Tina but she hasn't shown up. If she comes in, would you please tell her I had to leave? I'm on my lunch break and I need to get back to work." I was attempting to preserve the case and cast doubt on my actions so the subject would not know that I was law enforcement.

After leaving the store I radioed back to the all male team and was told they were almost back to Albuquerque. The supervisor had called off the surveillance from the office. I was horrified. My life was possibly in danger and my team left me there face to face with the subject of a drug investigation. Agents later laughed about that situation.

◆ I was "partnered" with a senior agent on a drug investigation which culminated in the arrest of several individuals. There were over a dozen agents at the scene the night of the arrests. As we were leaving the location, the senior agent backed into another car with a loud crash which gave both of us quite a jolt. I offered to get accident report documents out of my briefcase but the senior agent only laughed at me and drove away. He said that was what the FBI calls "regular wear and tear." In the "real" world – that's called <u>hit and run</u>.

♦   The most senior drug agent in Albuquerque was a known alcoholic and his breath reeked of cigarettes and alcohol from the earliest of morning encounters. All the agents that knew him, as well as the supervisors and upper management, were aware he had a severe drinking problem. At the FBI Academy, we had Ethics classes that emphasized that kind of behavior would not be tolerated . . . agents with drinking problems need to be reported and get help. In the field . . . an agent drinking was considered . . . no problem! Several agents were upset that this drunken agent got angry on the street and drew his gun on innocent civilians. Because no one was shot, it was not seen as a problem and he was never reprimanded nor did he ever receive "help." In fact it is bizarre that a lot of the agents (especially new agents) looked up to this guy.

He was a Training Agent (TA) and indoctrinated all the new drug squad agents with ways to "screw the system" and bang the books. In fact, it was commonplace for him to round up the entire drug squad and leave around 3:00 p.m. to go get a "pop" – his terminology for hitting the bars and drinking. Never mind that there are strict policies that agents are not to drink and drive, specifically their FBI vehicles - remember that "Bright Line?" In the field it was nothing more than a faded shadow.

♦   Two senior agents also had their own spin on the Field Office PT Test. While most agents were being timed as they ran around a track (six times to equal one and a half miles), these two walked, talked and laughed as they slowly sauntered one time around the track. One even smoked cigarettes as he walked. It would be interesting to see how these agents' FBI files were "padded" to get away with their blatant actions against FBI policy. They simply justified that they were . . . "participating."

♦   During a kidnapping case, the Assistance Special Agent in Charge (ASAC - #2 in the office) asked me to coordinate deployment of the SWAT team, pilots and additional agent and support personnel. I also assisted in the arrest of several subjects as they arrived at a restaurant and escorted the subject vehicle to the Albuquerque office.

With the assistance of an agent standing guard, I processed one of the subjects (fingerprints, photographs, documentation). Because of the late hour, pizza had been delivered and I took food to the subject before the interview was conducted. I was severely reprimanded by fellow agents for giving the subject food. I was told that people "like him" don't deserve to eat.

The FBI is required to keep a log of everything that happens when a subject is in custody. That means the time is documented for every bathroom break, food or drink provided, etc. I explained that if the FBI gave any appearance of mistreatment, the subject may claim that information was coerced and it could not be used in court, even a confession. I was criticized for attempting to preserve the integrity of the case. I must've missed the law that allows agents to be judge and jury. I understood my job to be investigating and apprehending subjects . . . the courts (justice system) having the responsibility to try, convict and sentence bad guys.

SETTING THE FOUNDATION

SA Haney was assigned as my TA when I arrived in Albuquerque. He's a good SA but a terrible TA. TAs are senior agents assigned (though some feel burdened) with a new agent for a number of weeks. A "good" TA will help set a solid FBI Field foundation for a new agent . . . assist with acclimation . . . and set the course for successful investigations. That is, TAs with an interest in "helping." SA Haney just stacked numerous (about 16) cases on my desk and told me to "call if you have any questions."

Now, as you can imagine, it's quite difficult to ask a question if you don't even know where to start with a case. Without the benefit of a TA that cared, much less made any effort to help, I did extensive research of previous cases and went to the FBI manuals detailing how to investigate each violation. It's very much like reading a computer programming book to figure out how to type a letter. You can get the information through exhaustive efforts, time and frustration . . . or someone can sit down with you and help explain the process.

I learned very quickly that SAs don't want to help each other. They exist as crabs in a bucket! If one starts doing well, the others will pull him back down to the bottom. If they all worked together, each could get out of the bucket and experience a tremendous environment . . . but they're just not smart enough to do that.

In the Field Office environment, the senior agents kept information to themselves, or in many cases, just didn't know the answer. Many new agents (including me) heard, "I'm not gonna do your work for you, go look it up." I think it was an attempt for them to feel superior and build themselves up while demeaning the new agents. What I came to understand is that it was all a game of smoke and mirrors, as well as pure laziness. These agents hadn't learned how to conduct in-depth investigations and passed cases off for newer agents to do the work, all before they were "found out." An in-depth FBI audit by an outside agency would likely discover the dead wood agents that have taken up space (and money) for decades.

I understand that camaraderie is important and there may be some "fudge factor" in everything . . . I'm all for that. However, blatant deception and laziness is hard to swallow. It's quite a talent for many agents to work so incredibly hard at doing nothing . . . and it was difficult not to notice when I was sitting in the same cubicle (four agents to a cubicle).

To give you an example of only one (of too many to list), an agent consistently came into the office around 7:30 (which is unusual), drank coffee and read the newspaper until ~ 9:00 (not so unusual). He shined his shoes at his desk and then changed clothes and left to work out until about 11:00. Then he was back in the office discussing where he wanted to go for lunch for the next 30 minutes. He would leave with a group of male agents around 11:30 and come back about 2:00 (the FBI SA lunch break is supposed to be 45 minutes – not two and a half hours). From 2:00 until 3:00 (sometimes 3:30) he would make telephone calls. Not that he would speak to anyone. On average, he talked to maybe one or two people per day. He spent the rest of his time shooting the breeze with other agents. By 4:00, he was out the door with the ever-used agent lingo, "Gotta check a lead."

I found that the most talented of new agents, hugely successful in their previous careers - scientists, engineers, high level managers, etc., were addressed in a condescending manner and looked down on. I accepted the challenge and diversity of my new assignments, dug in and worked hard. Although the new agent probation period is two years with a multitude of tasks and operations required, I completed everything necessary and was removed from probation four months early. You'd think that would be acknowledged as a positive accomplishment. Not in the FBI. I was ridiculed by male agents as being a "blue flamer," a negative term used to describe someone accomplishing great things and being on a career fast track. My squad-mates routinely told me, "Slow down, you're making us look bad" with them betting on how fast I would escalate to management.

Supervisors don't like to be wrong so when they give dim-witted directions, most agents simply nod their heads face-to-face and then disregard what they're told. I believe in communicating, understanding and learning. Although I was looking to my supervisor, TA and senior agents for guidance and direction, I quickly found that many of these agents were lacking in logical thinking and practical skills. I believed and trusted that these experienced SAs and SSAs knew what they were doing. I was proven time and again to be wrong. These were simply big boys playing "FBI" and trying to act important.

BANK ROBBERY

Within the first month of arrival in the Albuquerque Division, I responded to a bank robbery called over the radio at 5:30 on a Friday afternoon. We were told during new agent training at Quantico that every agent should respond when they hear of a bank robbery, especially in smaller divisions – Albuquerque certainly qualified as small with less than 60 agents. The only experience I had with bank robberies was that from the FBI Academy where I was assigned to evidence collection and fingerprinting. However, I was confident that other experienced agents would be on scene and I could assist as needed.

I was the only agent at the bank for over an hour, despite two telephone calls to the Albuquerque office requesting assistance. I conducted all interviews, retrieved the robbery note, bait money list, video, etc. and called again for assistance. SA Jenner (a white female who has since resigned from the FBI) arrived on scene with little added experience with bank robberies, so I again requested a senior agent on scene. After thinking we would be spending the night at the bank, SA Goomer arrived, reviewed the investigation conducted and released the scene.

My fellow squad-mates repeatedly stated that they would not respond to bank robberies because it was not "their job." I was ridiculed for assisting "other" agents.

FIRST WEEKEND DUTY

As the weekend complaint duty agent, the night desk personnel called me regarding a kidnapping so, as required, I notified the Reactive Squad supervisor, SSA Shive (since removed from the FBI). He was drunk at a party and screamed, "What the **** do you want me to do about it!" After I got over the shock of being yelled at, I reached out to another supervisor who helped resolve the situation. His response to my encounter with SSA Shive was (without batting an eye), "Yep, that's how he is."

BLIND LEADING THE BLIND

Within approximately two months of arriving in Albuquerque, the WCC Squad had four experienced agents leave the Squad. Agents remaining included three agents newly transferred from other squads, two agents with one year of FBI experience, two first office probationary transfers from Quantico (me for one), and one mid-level SA. The decision to comprise a squad in this manner left the "blind leading the blind" with no experienced WCC agent base to draw on. The agents were extremely dissatisfied and continually voiced discontentment with their positions, management, and the FBI as a whole. Rather than accept the situation, buckle down, learn their job and become an expert – they moaned and groaned to each other about how bad they had it.

FBI GRIPING

♦ You'd think FBI SAs would find something good about what they do, about the difference they make and the privilege and honor they have in serving their country. I sure believed that . . . until I stepped inside the FBI.

It was a regular practice for agents to criticize the squad supervisors, Albuquerque Division Management, and the FBI Headquarters (FBI HQ) Management to include the Director. It absolutely shocked me that agents managed to voice critical, derogatory statements regarding the majority of agents, to include each other if not present.

I went to lunch with a group of about 12 agents on two occasions. The first turned out to be a total "***** session." Agents made negative comments about everyone and everything. I defended agents not present, and even people I didn't know, suggesting alternative scenarios than the outlandish attacks discussed . . . definitely not a way to be popular. Afterward, I thought maybe it had just been a bad day (still giving the benefit of the doubt). I went one more time and the biting, mean comments were even worse. It's difficult to forget something that is said and I felt it was unproductive to be poisoned against individuals before even working with them. I found most of those agents were pleasant individually but fed on negativity when put together.

♦ It wasn't long before I found myself in the center of a heated exchange with an older agent I'll call Bob. He came to our squad area attracting about eight agents with his tirade. He had applied for the position of media liaison and was furious that the position was given to the Albuquerque Chief Division Counsel (CDC) who had been unofficially filling the position for months. He said the CDC was an idiot that couldn't do his job and the only reason he got the position was because he was a drinking buddy with upper management. The CDC was never in the office and Bob was outraged over the situation.

Having been in Public Relations at TRW, I commented that the CDC could only do his job by being face-to-face building media relationships. I also asked if Bob had any Public Relations experience. Bob turned on me like a snake. He continued his rant which soon became a blasting of the entire FBI. I then asked him a question that I have since asked myself on numerous occasions . . . if it's so bad and you're that unhappy, why don't you just leave? Life is too short to be miserable.

* COMIC RELIEF *

The Albuquerque CDC held the media liaison position for several years and has claim to one of the funniest Albuquerque live-feed media moments. The local media set up an interview in the building courtyard in front of a large water fall and fountain. Only the camera man was on site asking the CDC for information regarding an FBI case. Before either of them could react, a homeless woman stripped down and emerged from the fountain, charging up behind the CDC in all her glory for the live audience to see. The TV station made numerous copies and distributed them so the CDC never lived it down.

♦ A difficult adjustment to the FBI work atmosphere was the common and daily use of extremely foul language. In each of my previous professional workplaces, I sometimes heard a word here or there to spice things up or make a point. However, I had never been saturated by such constant vulgarity. Unfortunately, what you're around rubs off and I found myself quickly cursing like a crude sailor . . . not a proud accomplishment.

♦ I coined a term for the agent dynamic in the Albuquerque office - "Cubicle Bomb." One person would have an issue, perhaps a legitimate situation that they just needed to talk through and vent. Another person would interject how outrageous that situation was and bring in a different personal scenario that was even worse. Then a third person would chime in with additional comments and escalate the discussion to an outright "***** session," which was my cue to leave. If you looked hard enough, you could probably see the mushroom cloud left by these "Cubicle Bombs" and sadly, these "sessions" would often continue for five to eight hours, almost <u>every day</u>! The fact that these agents were not producing work speaks directly to the lack of FBI management.

I had never been exposed to such a negative working environment and the stress of that environment proved to be detrimental. In my previous career with TRW, I remember crying on two occasions. The first when my grandmother died, the second when my dog died. I don't believe in being "emotional" in the workplace, but I found myself on many occasions barely making it to the exit door at the end of the day before the flood of tears came. After some time with no relief, I discussed the working environment with SSA Mocha, my very arrogant and unresponsive supervisor.

He failed to even address the problem. Seeing no alternative, I worked to resolve the situation as best I could. The Electronic Technicians (ETs) provided me with a cigarette lighter adapter outlet so I could plug in my laptop computer and work in my Bureau vehicle to write unclassified reports.

I continued to remain positive, conducted investigations, and wrote my reports in the Bureau vehicle to lessen time in the office. I was cordial with my squad mates but when a "***** session" started, I left the area . . . which meant I was out of the office . . . a lot. After a period of time, SSA Mocha asked how my reports were being completed since he didn't see me in the office for long periods of time. We again discussed the negative working environment. He said he'd been busy and hadn't had time to work on any problems and he felt bad that I had to take the steps of changing my work area to a car. I told him that it would be fine to put my computer "in the restroom," but I simply could not work in the present environment.

Eventually our squad was relocated to a new office with more space. It allowed for fewer agents in each cubicle but the working environment as related to the "***** sessions" did not lessen, but rather worsened. A major point of contention was that we were moved into a "condemned" building - literally. The top floors of this building were uninhabitable and we were given instruction on where heavy safes and stacks of paper could be stored so the floor would not collapse.

Removing myself from the "***** sessions" was helpful but also very isolating. Thinking that the poisonous attitudes of these agents may be exclusively a "squad" problem and seeing no improvement for almost two years, I took the initiative to request a transfer to another squad. SSA Mocha told me that he supported my transfer but nothing happened for almost a year. I later discovered that he reported to upper management that I couldn't be transferred because of my case load.

I also used another method of coping called TDY/Training. I volunteered for every out of office training or assignment that was offered. Besides learning a lot, it gave me reprieve from the oppressive office environment and the opportunity to work some interesting cases, like Eric Rudolph (Olympic Park Bomber), one of the largest cases in the Bureau.

JUST SAY NO

♦ I soon learned that some male agents had the option to work only cases they deemed interesting. Where I was assigned a variety of violations and cooperated with my supervisor and his instruction/assignments, other agents threw temper tantrums in his office, screaming and swearing at SSA Mocha that they wouldn't work certain cases. Because SSA Mocha could not resolve conflict, his resolution was to do as he was told and cower to the demands of his subordinates. An added benefit for me . . . I received the additional cases "declined" by the disgruntled agents.

♦ One "no" that I did express caused venom for years to come. Patty, the only other female agent on my squad, was very open about being a lesbian. This caused disgusting derogatory discussions among the male agents, emphasized with crude hand and mouth gestures. I remained professional with Patty but declined her numerous invitations to after work activities and functions - which made her mad . . . very mad. She went on a personal crusade to slander me in any way she could . . . to anyone that would listen, including SSA Mocha.
I later learned that she tried to get agents to do surveillance on me because she didn't know where I was. She also rummaged through my desk when I was out of the office.

♦ A federal security guard who knew me as an FBI SA ran up to me in a panic. I could only presume there was a pressing matter at hand and I began to scan the area as she talked. I was more than shocked when she wanted to know how I'd feel if I were to be asked out by a woman. I had been chased down on a city street by a professional whose job it was to keep our federal building safe, asking if I was a lesbian and then being told that the guards were making bets about me. "Inappropriate" doesn't even begin to explain this situation and I can't tell you how uncomfortable it was to pass by these guards each day that followed. I discussed this incident with SSA Mocha and true to form, he did nothing.

♦ When two FBI agents were involved in a bank robbery case shooting, our squad was having a breakfast meeting several minutes from the shooting location. SSA Mocha was paged with information about the situation and the squad immediately left to assist. Radio traffic was disorganized and the SWAT team was put on stand-by. The entire situation was chaotic and two of our agents needed immediate assistance.

After the scene was cleared, I transported the agents involved to the office and stayed with Jimmy for over two hours to assure his mental stability. I was then tasked to administer the Victim/Witness program to all those affected by the shooting. Numerous other agents were on hand but they didn't know what to do. They simply ignored the shooting victims/witnesses and waited for me to get there. I then assisted the Evidence Response Team (ERT) in processing the crime scene.

I believed Jimmy and I had a good working relationship and he was appreciative of my assistance to him during the shooting incident. He had been extremely shaken with the reality that he narrowly escaped death, even getting marks on his hand when he grabbed the hammer of the subject's gun as it was fired into a room. Jimmy spoke candidly about his fears regarding the shooting and about his wife and newborn twins. After that day Jimmy often greeted me with a polite hug.

On one occasion, Jimmy kissed me on the lips in the gated agent parking area. He was completely out of line and I pulled away from him in disbelief. I knew Jimmy was going through a difficult time but his actions upset me to the point that I spoke to a supervisor I trusted about what happened. The supervisor strongly suggested I file a complaint against Jimmy. I didn't want to add stress to his situation and get him in trouble; I just didn't want it to happen again. The supervisor didn't think Jimmy should get a "free feel" and was disappointed that I did not go forward with a complaint.

It became clear that I was in a no win situation regardless of what I did. In subsequent encounters with Jimmy, I positioned myself away from him and was confident that he understood his actions were inappropriate and unwelcome. However, a short time later, Jimmy began to snub me and that quickly escalated to badmouthing and calling me a ***** to numerous agents. I did nothing but help this man through a difficult situation and restrained from filing a complaint against him, yet his malice continued to the day I left the Albuquerque division.

SUPERVISOR SUPPORT FACADE

♦ SA reports must be painstakingly accurate for testimony in court. I took this responsibility very seriously and required complete truthfulness and accuracy in my reporting (as should all FBI SAs). I remember a supervisor unable to find fault with my investigations, often criticized my reports for being too detailed. He spent an inordinate amount of time playing a game of unnecessary revisions on my reports. When he could find nothing wrong with a document, he would reword sections where I would have to explain how he had changed the entire meaning and I could not sign as to its content, much less testify to his inaccuracies. In retrospect, this was a game he played only with me. Another agent on my squad told me he had never seen anyone treated in that manner.

♦ I discussed the strategy of a high level Healthcare Fraud case with SSA Mocha who advised that an undercover case should be implemented. I did not agree with going forward with this strategy due to safety considerations for the undercover personnel and extensive backstopping (historical information needed to support an undercover operative), but I considered his instruction and did the necessary research.

Without my knowledge, SSA Mocha repeatedly reported to upper management that I was working an undercover operation – big kudos for his squad. I prepared the necessary documentation, conducted the appropriate inquiries regarding backstopping and showed emphatically that an undercover operation was neither feasible nor appropriate. SSA Mocha made himself look good to upper management and then threw me under the bus when I "didn't deliver." The truth is that I never thought an undercover operation would work in this case and produced the evidence to prove it wouldn't work. SSA Mocha also enlisted the assistance of the FBI HQ Health Care Fraud Unit which, for all intents and purposes, brought the local investigation to a political stand still. SSA Mocha then criticized me for not moving this investigation forward.

♦ For another high level Healthcare Fraud case, I discussed with SSA Mocha the strategy of obtaining records through subpoena vs. search warrant. Issues of concern included whether it was critical that the records not be altered. One of my informants provided information that the subject would most likely alter or destroy the records if they were requested.

After in-depth discussions, SSA Mocha and I agreed on subpoena - that despite any alteration or destruction, Medicare guidelines requiring an agency to maintain these records would suffice regardless of the condition of the documents. Then, after SSA Mocha considered how much attention the squad would receive from upper management by having an "operation," he directed me to obtain these documents via search warrant.

I again complied with his instruction and worked tirelessly to prepare a search warrant, search plan, personnel plan and schedule to proceed. I was then assigned to a 30-day TDY for an FBI major case in Birmingham. I worked the allocated core hours for the TDY investigation and when I returned to my temporary residence, worked on the search warrant with the continued instruction of an Assistant United States Attorney (AUSA). I completed the TDY assignment, received a letter of commendation, and was requested to return for another TDY. As soon as I arrived in Albuquerque, the Healthcare Fraud search warrant was finalized and approved by the AUSA. I was then advised that a meeting was necessary with the Supervisory AUSA (S/AUSA), me and SSA Mocha.

At this meeting, the S/AUSA suggested we (the FBI) consider requesting the records by subpoena. SSA Mocha immediately replied that subpoena would be a good course of action, leaving the impression that I had been unfounded in pursuing a search warrant even though I acted on his direct instruction.

SSA Mocha also reported to FBI upper management that there was a change in focus on this case. As documented to FBI HQ when I opened the case, the focus of this investigation never changed.

♦ As a member of the National Infrastructure Protection Center (NIPC), I was assigned a laptop computer with an internal modem. I approached SSA Mocha regarding the need for an external hard drive to comply with FBI policy that no FBI material be on a hard drive connected to the Internet. A separate hard drive was required and I provided SSA Mocha with an order page identifying the drive necessary and the associated cost. Simple! SSA Mocha said he would have to coordinate with the computer specialists to get the hard drive. I followed up with SSA Mocha about this on four separate occasions and was told that he had not gotten around to it, but would. After repeatedly asking over several months, I abandoned the inquiries and he never got to it.

♦ Peter, an agent and fellow NIPC member, contacted me by telephone and asked to borrow my laptop computer. In the spirit of teamwork, I placed the computer in Peter's chair the following day. After approximately two weeks, I called and requested the computer be returned. Peter replied that he had put the computer on his property list and it now belonged to him. I was taken aback and objected, stating that his request was to "borrow" the computer - not take it. I needed it returned. Peter said that SSA Mocha told him he could have it. I approached SSA Mocha about this incident and he denied giving Peter permission to take the computer. He told me that he'd like to handle the situation . . . which is to say that he did nothing.

I advised Peter that there were computer files that I needed so he and another male agent downloaded files to a disk and tossed it on my desk, laughing as they walked away. It is inconceivable that an agent can "take" something, fill out a property sheet, and it becomes their property. I was never even notified of this change by the property custodian, who had a property sheet on file that the computer was assigned to me. The difficulty for me was what to do about a situation where again, I was humiliated and my supervisor seemed to be at the root of it. How do you handle blatant disrespect?

My father suggested I file an EEO complaint against SSA Mocha. He had been upset for quite a while about the way I was being treated and was confident that SSA Mocha would never treat any of the male agents in that manner. I didn't want to make waves so I swallowed my pride once again and kept working to the best of my ability.

♦ There were also incidents of such pettiness that I was reminded of kindergarten. My desk area was located adjacent to Greg (remember the guy stealing your money)? From the time I arrived in Albuquerque, he put ink block stamps between us for dual use because they were used intermittently when documents were completed. This continued for months. One day when I came into the cubical area, I found the usual scene of three agents laughing and hanging out. I printed out a document and attempted to locate the block stamp. Greg snapped at me, "Go get your own stamp." I have no idea what prompted Greg's behavior but I left the cubical area to get a stamp from the supply room. As I walked away I heard them laughing and realized it was just an opportunity to embarrass and harass me. It was so ridiculous that grown men, and FBI SAs to boot, would delight in such nonsense.

♦ During an SOM operation, the team was to set up on a residence early in the morning. After an initial meeting in a parking lot, several agents went to pick up bagels at a shop adjacent to the meeting area. The team leader and I immediately went to the residence to set up. The subject was already moving and the team leader called on the radio for additional help. It took an inordinate amount of time before any other agents responded so the two of us were left doing the job of an entire team (6 – 8 agents). When the other agents were finally contacted, they were asked where they had been. They responded they were eating bagels. The team leader told them that we were working and they should've gotten the bagels "to go." One of the agents laughed and said, "Oh, you said get them to go? We thought you said eat them slow." It was a funny comment, but the issue was never addressed that these agents disregarded direct instruction and were lackadaisical and remiss about doing their job.

NO NONSENSE SAFETY

♦ On several occasions, the Albuquerque office was evacuated due to bomb threats. During one such incident, I was entering the building from the parking area and an agent leaving told me about the situation. Had I not encountered that agent, I would've entered the building with no awareness of the danger present. I suggested to SSA Mocha that an "All Agent" page be set up for situations like this. In that way, every agent would know of the immediate situation and be alert to possible suspects or packages. SSA Mocha did not address this so I made the same suggestion to the Bomb Specialist, the Weapons of Mass Destruction Coordinator, and the ETs (who set up the paging system). No action was ever taken.

♦ During another incident information was passed, word of mouth, to evacuate due to a bomb threat. I made a sweep through the office to ensure that all personnel were aware of the evacuation (to include interview rooms and restrooms). I told the dispatcher that he needed to evacuate. He stated that the ASAC told him to stay. I suggested he evacuate and monitor radio traffic from the offsite location one block away. I was appalled that the upper management placed him in danger. In the event that an explosion did occur, I would find it extremely difficult to explain to his family why everyone else was evacuated and he was told to stay, especially since other options were available to assure his safety.

♦ Because of the danger of a truck bomber driving up and blowing up an FBI building, requirements were put in place that every FBI building was to have a 100 foot set back from the street. That requirement was impossible in most downtown areas so each FBI Division was to make appropriate adjustments. In Albuquerque, the upper management first did nothing and then made a ridiculous decision after a visit from Director Louis Freeh. The office space included a bridge over a downtown city street. FBI files and employees were literally sitting over the street. A bomber could easily abandon a vehicle and blow up the building. The Director identified this as a *serious safety concern* that was to be *addressed immediately*. Reasoning that a bomb would blast only in a vertical direction, the Albuquerque management simply moved the employees to the edge of the bridge overhang. Bombs blow as they will in any and all directions. Years later and well after 9/11 the city street was blocked off which finally addressed this safety issue.

♦ When two FBI agents were involved in a shooting, SSA Mocha was paged and given information about the situation. Radio traffic was disorganized and chaotic. An "All Agent" paging system would notify every agent within approximately 30 seconds that "Agent shooting in progress at x and y - Respond Immediately", or check with supervisor, or get to an area and wait for instruction. Indeed, an agent was in the immediate area of the shooting and learned of it through an Albuquerque Police Officer he was with. Agents need to trust, with absolute certainty, that additional agents are on the way when help is needed. Throughout four years of disorganized situations I experienced, there was never a system implemented to alert All Agents of immediate danger.

DOUBLE STANDARD

◆ I applied for Government Employment Training Association (GETA) funds for an Abnormal Behavior class given at the University of New Mexico. I was told by others that had received these funds that mine was a legitimate request as related to my work as an FBI SA and my future aspirations to work in the Behavior Analysis Unit (BAU). I wrote and submitted the GETA form to the SAC for approval and signature. The SAC returned the form and asked for documentation to justify the class. I obliged him and wrote in detail about my experience, how the class applies to my current responsibilities, and how it applies to future FBI goals.

The form was again returned, unsigned, and my supervisor told me that the SAC did not like the tone of the document. He said that it read as if an attorney wrote it (I question if other documents written by male agents have been characterized in this way). Even after revision, the SAC refused to sign it and would not give a reason. I asked to have this reviewed by FBI HQ. When I followed up on my request, I was told that paperwork and original receipts had been lost. I re-faxed the entire package to FBI HQ and finally got their approval. My concern was in the battle. GETA funds are available for all federal employees and classes of this type had been approved for male agents in the past. I was forced to battle to enhance my skills and value for use by the FBI.

◆ A supervisor and AUSA directed that certain evidence be handled with gloves to protect fingerprint identification. I worked with the assistance of numerous support personnel to prepare this evidence for trial. The Case Agent entered the room and started to review the evidence. I told him that we were given explicit instructions to handle the evidence with gloves. The agent indignantly replied that he would not use gloves, they wouldn't send the evidence for analysis anyway, and proceeded to go through the evidence.

♦ On the Wen Ho Lee (WHL) case, the largest FCI case in the FBI, I completed more investigative leads than any other agent, was the Case Agent for two FCI spin off cases, gave daily briefings to FBI HQ, was the SOM team leader and I was tasked by the SAC (during the proceedings) to create the WHL debriefing video for use by the FBI Director to present before Congress. I was given no budget, no script and no assistance. Thankfully I have a solid background in film so I immediately started filming everything possible, a completely backward process to starting with a script for filming. After writing the script with an ET and getting approval to travel to FBI HQ to edit the video, I requested (on numerous occasions) to meet with the two Case Agents for their input. I felt a meeting was critical to understand the product they desired rather than only my input. Over the next three weeks, both agents told me they were too busy to look at the script.

I had no choice but to ask the SAC for his review of the script and approval. I spent almost two weeks at FBI HQ working many nights until 2:00 a.m. (I knew the time because the Metro had already stopped running and hailing a cab in downtown DC at that hour was difficult). I was the videographer, director, editor and narrator. The SAC said that the video was exceptional. He had seen similar projects from New York and other divisions that paled in comparison to this product.

The video has also been lauded by the Albuquerque US Attorney's office, Washington Headquarter personnel from the Department of Justice and Department of Energy, as well as FBI HQ and other FBI Divisions. Although male agents received substantial cash awards for their "exceptional performance" in the WHL case with much less contribution, I received a certificate of appreciation for my "exceptional performance." I did ensure that the FBI HQ personnel that assisted in this project received letters of commendation and time-off awards.

♦ I was clear on my duties and responsibilities as an SA and I took them very seriously. I was one of the few. When returning to the office from a lunch break, I encountered a robbery in progress. The subject was running through an intersection followed by a store manager. I followed the subject into a neighborhood where he had a gang waiting and they were beating the store manager. There was no time to call for back-up, this man was being pulverized. I only had a moment to say, "God help me" and He was listening. I broke up the fight, arrested the subject, recovered the stolen merchandise and called for the Albuquerque Police Department to transport and process the subject. I also made sure to tell the store manager that nothing material is worth his life. He should never have confronted the robber.

I completed an arrest report when I got back to the office. I admit that I was expecting to be told I did a good job . . . that it took a lot of guts (and bravery) to do what I did. That never happened. I was quickly deflated when two senior SAs laughed at me and said that in time I would learn to look the other way. I stood there in disbelief . . . appalled, shocked and disappointed. I put myself at risk when I stepped in and helped an innocent person that was being physically harmed during a crime – who knows if he would've been killed had I not been there. I did the right thing! Even regarding the responsibility to the public, what agents are charged to do (on the books) is very different than what they will actually do in the field. Although many agents received commendations for minimal assistance to local law enforcement, it's no big surprise that I did not receive any recognition for this arrest.

No matter what the situation, no matter how well I did my job - it seemed to always come with an awful, lingering aftertaste.

I don't remember the first day suicidal thoughts entered my mind. I only remember joking with family members that Moses wandered around the desert for 40 years . . . I had two down, only thirty eight to go. By the fall of 1999, I was entertaining the idea of getting all my important papers in order, putting them on the kitchen table and going out in the back yard with a sheet and my gun. I could cover myself with the sheet and tuck it under me so it would stay in place. By lying down in the grass, parallel with the brick of my house, there would be no damage if the bullet passed through my head and hit the brick. Whoever found me would not have to witness a messy scene; they would just see the sheet and call for help. Clean up would be no problem . . . just hose down the grass.

I never took action toward that plan and I credit that to God's grace and some very sensitive and obedient Christians. Most of my evenings at that time consisted of crying and smoking. I kept on a good face when I was away from my house so no one knew I was deeply hurting and that I had lost hope. Even as I write this I keep thinking - it's just a job! I'm a vibrant, intelligent woman . . . but I was also brainwashed into believing what the American people and the FBI told me - the FBI is the best! No matter how awful it was, anything else would be a major step down and I would be a disappointment to everyone that knew me. I've heard people say that suicide is selfish and you will go to hell but I can tell you that my thoughts were only on stopping the pain . . . and I know that the only unpardonable sin is blasphemy against the Holy Spirit - I just wanted to be with my Lord.

Therefore I tell you, every sin and blasphemy (every evil, abusive, injurious speaking, or indignity against sacred things) can be forgiven men, but blasphemy against the [Holy] Spirit shall not and cannot be forgiven. Matthew 12:31 (AMP)

God has a great plan for me to accomplish <u>on this earth</u> and He was not about to let Satan snatch me from fulfilling that plan.

The thief comes only to steal and kill and destroy; I have come that they may have life, and have it to the full.
John 10:10 (NIV)

At the time, I didn't realize how subtly Satan had moved me into isolation. I've often told of checking your life temperature with the frog story (I also collect frogs for their acronym **F**ully **R**ely **O**n **G**od). If you put a frog in a pot of boiling water, it will jump out to escape danger. But if you put a frog in a pot of cool water and then – *very, very slowly,* turn up the heat – the frog's body adjusts to the temperature and can boil to death before it even realizes it's in danger.

The same can happen for any of us if we are not checking our life temperature. God's people seldom make giant leaps into negative situations. For example, if you ask a church pastor if he would ever have an affair . . . he will likely respond *absolutely not.* Now add an attractive woman going through a crisis. The pastor may offer to listen, pray and offer comfort, even a hug. The temperature of the situation may start to rise when meetings are moved outside an office setting, maybe for lunch or dinner. Neither person began with inappropriate intentions . . . but soon emotions become involved and the situation "boils" to the point of a full blown affair. I know of a pastor that guards against that very thing by never closing the door when he counsels a woman. Some men will not eat any meal with a woman other than their wives. I applaud them for setting strict boundaries.

This same methodology applies to my situation. If you asked me when I began my FBI career if I would ever consider suicide, I would emphatically say *absolutely not*! But when you factor in extreme disappointment with the FBI, I wasn't going to church, I wasn't reading my Bible and my prayers were just intermittent cries for help - it's easier to understand. I am thankful that God knew my heart and knew how to get me through that time by encouraging me through family and long time friends. In the midst of my lowest days I would receive a card or a phone call. I had known Ester for over ten years and she told me that God tugged on her heart to keep sending me cards with Biblical Scriptures of hope. It was no coincidence that I received those messages on the most difficult days. I had known Terry for over twelve years and though there was a period that we hadn't been close, God nudged him to call me on numerous occasions when my world was covered in darkness. My sister also knew the ugly details and helped to lift me out of the black pits.

It was during that time that I was diagnosed with Mononucleosis and two months later went through two surgeries for kidney stones. It fascinates me that dealing with health issues got my mind off suicide. It also gave me a break from the hateful agents I encountered daily and put me in an environment to be nurtured and comforted. The medical staff was compassionate and caring and Elaine came to the rescue on more than one occasion when I needed help . . . even taking me to the hospital at 2:00 a.m. when I was doubled over in pain. You know you have a true friend when they stand by you while you throw up your toenails.

It would have been easy to think God was punishing me in some way or making my life even more difficult. However, by the time the medical issues were over, I was with my family for the Christmas holiday and I realized that the suicidal thoughts were a thing of the past. No matter how difficult life may be . . . things will change. Suicide is a permanent solution to a temporary problem.

"Character cannot be developed in ease and quiet. Only through experiences of trial and suffering can the soul be strengthened, vision cleared, ambition inspired and success achieved." ~ Helen Keller

❧ *6* ❧

Finding My Voice
&
Going Into Battle

"The nail that sticks up gets hammered down."
~ Japanese Proverb

❧❧❧❧❧❧

Many people prepared for Y2K to bring chaos and destruction. For me it came like a breath of fresh air. I was transferred to work FCI, I ended a very unhealthy relationship and worked with the first (of only three), good FBI supervisors I would have in my nine year career.

Barry was a stately man, spoke fluent Mandarin Chinese and was brought in as a supervisor from the FBI Los Angeles office to untangle the mess made of the WHL case. I was brought in after the comedy of errors - started by the ASAC. It is my understanding that the Albuquerque office was given monies dedicated to fund two full time agents on the case. The ASAC decided to assign those agents to Indian Reservation crimes and he left an agent I'll call Ross as the WHL lone ranger. The problem . . . Ross was more than odd – he clearly suffered from Obsessive Compulsive Disorder (OCD) and though he was a very kind man, his behaviour was bizarre. Rather than offering to get him help, the agents working in his area only made things worse by heightening his anxiety.

For example, Ross had a ritual at the end of each day. He deliberately and meticulously placed each object on his desk at a right angle, put all paperwork away, checked his safe, used the restroom, checked his safe again, checked that all objects were at right angles and then left for the day. Agents took great pleasure in slightly moving objects on his desk when he went to the restroom so he would repeat his ritual or wait until he reached the elevator and ask if his safe was locked (so he'd again start over with his end of day ritual). It appeared that Ross was more preoccupied with his issues than with handling our national security.

Things only got worse when the SAC heavy-handedly ordered a female agent to threaten WHL during an interrogation by discussing the Rosenberg's (electrocuted for not cooperating with the federal government in an espionage case).

Needless to say, the case did not progress. It was only when information was *brought* to the FBI that the WHL case spun up to a FBI Major Case Investigation - which meant agents were assigned on a TDY basis from Albuquerque (me included among only a handful) and numerous other FBI divisions. It was like a bee hive of activity and I found it refreshing to work with professionals that were focused on doing the work of the FBI (though I can't condone the vast majority of decisions made by FBI upper management in the WHL case). I'll never forget a TDY supervisor commenting that he was shocked by what he witnessed in the Albuquerque personnel. He said that I (and one other male agent) definitely did not belong in Albuquerque - we were great agents and much too professional to be there.

Barry and I worked together well professionally and became friends. Barry also accepted a transfer to Albuquerque as the FCI supervisor and he treated each employee with fairness and respect. As time went on, Barry became aware of the difficulties I had experienced and told me to document everything. I had done some personal "journaling" about how I felt but I began to write about each incident. Though I never intended it for a specific purpose, it would prove to be invaluable in the years to come.

Once I had completed the documentation, I sat with Barry as he read and commented on the issues I endured since arriving in Albuquerque. He said two things that will always stay with me: 1) he got out a bundle of pencils and raised one in the middle to represent me. He said I did an excellent job and had a great attitude. Then he hit the bundle to level all the pencils and said as long as I was demonstrating excellence in the FBI, I would continue to be struck down, and 2) the battle I continued to fight (doing the right thing) had taken away my voice. Barry took the time to help build me up and reinforce that the problem was with the apathy, inappropriate actions and arrogance prevalent in Albuquerque, not with me.

It's very true that you sometimes can't see the forest for the trees. As I distanced myself from the events and got an overall perspective, I felt an unbelievable freedom and validation . . . and I got my voice back. I continued with a renewed vigour to be the very best I could be. I couldn't change the world or even Albuquerque - but I could make a difference in my cases and the people around me. After WHL was arrested and the bulk of the case was completed, there were only a handful of agents that remained on the squad. It looked like things were on the upswing – but it was only the calm before the storm. I was aware of a lot of wrongdoing in Albuquerque but it was so rampant I had never reported anything . . . that is until I was personally confronted by the ASAC.

I had been close with a SWAT member who had weapons stolen out of his truck so an Office of Professional Responsibility (OPR - the FBI's Internal Affairs) investigation was opened on the matter. He was very apprehensive about what would happen and asked me to go to lunch with him after he completed his interview with the FBI HQ investigators. We rode in his truck and he handed me his Signed Sworn Statement. As I read it, I realized he had lied about three events and the end of the Statement admonished him not to discuss this matter with anyone but the investigators. I was stunned! I tossed the document at him, upset that he would even show it to me and I told him he could be fired for lying. I suggested he go back and correct his statement before it went any further. He laughed and said the investigators were idiots and they would never know. I was angry that he had literally turned into one of "them" and said that if I was ever asked, I would not lie for him. He assured me that he would never ask me to lie . . . and I didn't mention the situation to anyone. Let me assure you - this man was not a "friend." A true friend will NOT put you in the position to "cover" or "lie" for them - - - because the right kind of friends will be living a life of truth.

I was still being called on to work SOM and the ASAC wanted me to work half-time FCI and half-time SOM. I knew that would be a formula for failure so we had a meeting and I requested to be assigned full-time to FCI - which eventually happened. I had a short reprieve and was able to enjoy my work, my supervisor and my squad.

The bottom would drop out in less than two months. The SWAT member had been involved with numerous "***** sessions" and the ASAC got wind that I knew something about the SWAT OPR. As the #2 man in charge, the ASAC was in a very powerful position, but he was also an overgrown kid. He often screamed at people (or at walls), stomped his feet, got red in the face and slammed doors. Simply put - he had temper tantrums like a three year old that were very intimidating coming from a grown man in his position.

I was in a meeting with Barry when the ASAC arrived and told me that he heard rumour that I had information about the SWAT OPR. He then adamantly stated that if I had any information I better come forward - I had a duty to report wrong-doing.

There was a deep moral dilemma with this situation. Of course, the FBI stands for Fidelity, Bravery and Integrity in everything - - - but the "Agent Code" is that you don't rat on your fellow agent. My character made it clear what I had to do but I confirmed my decision further with the FBI Manual of Administrative Operations and Procedures (MAOP) which spelled out in black and white my responsibility in reporting.

I set a meeting with Barry and told him what I knew. Everything surrounding OPR matters is "supposed" to be confidential but the FBI doesn't know what that word means. If the SAC and ASAC secretaries aren't gossiping in the break room - the management is having open discussions over their drinks after work. To make a very, very long story short . . . after a lot of paperwork, interviews and dealing with nasty comments and "go die" looks from fellow agents, the FBI reprimanded the SWAT member and put me under investigation. I was given 30 days off without pay because of misusing an FBI vehicle. I had been in the SWAT truck when I knew the agent had been using it as his personal vehicle. I also received an additional seven days off without pay for failing to report "in a timely manner." I was the only agent reprimanded though most of the Albuquerque Division knew he had misused his FBI vehicle for years. I was incredibly naïve to think that the FBI actually expected truth. In hindsight I understand what I was expected to do (even by FBI Headquarters). I was expected to say "I don't recall" . . . the pat answer given by agents at every level. The message was broadcast loud and clear - if you tell the truth you will be annihilated. Just as the FBI doesn't want to de-brief operations to identify problems . . . they don't want the truth in any other area.

- *Oh, and that SWAT member that lied? He was promoted to FBI Headquarters as a supervisor.*

The ASAC was aware of some of my difficulties with other agents since the OPR, even to the point of getting harassing notes on my car in the gated agent parking area. Rather than take any corrective action, he told me a story. He said that he was involved with a similar situation in a previous office where he was not well liked because he did his job and was not part of the "cool clique." He said that he addressed the problem by going to one of the sources and threatened to beat the hell out of him. I asked if that was how he wanted me to handle this, just to threaten other agents. He slumped in his chair and said he handled his situation badly and the FBI should have a higher standard (one of the few things he ever said that I agreed with).

By early 2001 Barry was transferred and I found myself with another inept supervisor. I was looking for a way out of Albuquerque. Barry and another FCI supervisor suggested and recommended me for the position of Relief Supervisor (RS). Although it is only a first step into FBI Management and you can have a frontal lobotomy and still get the position, that box must be checked before you can apply for FBI HQ positions. I didn't particularly want to work in Washington, DC again but I felt it had to be an improvement from my current environment.

Every FBI management position goes through a formal Career Board process where supervisors evaluate a candidate's knowledge, skills and abilities. This meeting is recorded on audio cassette (thanks to the Black Agents Don't Get Equality 'BADGE' 10-year class action lawsuit settlement). I was more than qualified for the RS position with a performance rating of "Superior" and it is an open position, meaning there is no limit to the number of agents selected - in fact, there had never been a case where a qualified agent had been denied the RS position . . . until me.

Barry was in that Career Board. He couldn't disclose the "confidential proceedings" but he did tell me the decision was definitely not based on my knowledge, skill and ability (which is FBI policy) and what happened was wrong! He strongly suggested I get a copy of the cassette tape through the Freedom Of Information Privacy Act (FOIPA). I immediately requested the tape and spoke with the EEO Counselor.

Without the RS position I could not apply for a transfer and I felt trapped. That realization threw me into a tailspin. There was a period of four days that I could not compose myself to go to work. I didn't have suicidal thoughts but I knew I needed help. I went to my doctor and was referred to a Christian Counselor. I still remember him asking what brought me to see him. "My give a **** factor is at zero." I was diagnosed with "Depression due to work-related stress." I didn't know how to resolve my situation and I couldn't make sound decisions until my emotions were in check. He suggested anti-depressants which I vehemently opposed. I was furious that the FBI had put me in a position to be "medicated." However, regardless of how I got there, I had to do everything I could to get healthy . . . and the medication was exactly what I needed.

I don't know what your objections may be if you find yourself in a situation where you need help, but I can tell you that anti-depressants didn't make me feel sluggish, weird or different. They simply took the edge off and helped me to clearly and objectively look at my situation. I also knew I wouldn't have to take them forever. Years later I learned that a great number of Albuquerque employees were taking anti-depressants.

With a fresh approach and a clear mind I realized that the Albuquerque Management was determined to keep me so they could beat me up for telling the truth. I felt the only resolution was the truth, the whole truth and nothing but the truth.

> *Then you will know the truth, and the truth will set you free.*
> *John 8:32 (NIV)*

I wrote a 45 page report to the SAC outlining my concerns regarding: 1) Safety Issues, 2) Harassment Issues, 3) Unprofessional Conduct, and I asked for a transfer out of the Albuquerque Division. The SAC read the report and told me he didn't feel it met the level of a transfer. I disagreed and told him I would need to take further action. I sent the report to the FBI HQ Ombudsman (in place to investigate complaints and resolve conflicts when chain-of-command is ineffective) and he soon called to discuss the serious issues I reported. He was very concerned about my situation and asked if he could show the report to the FBI Director. I gave him permission to show it to anyone that could help.

"Collective fear stimulates herd instinct, and tends to produce ferocity toward those who are not regarded as members of the herd." ~ Bertrand Russell

~ 7 ~

The Wreck That Saved My Life

"Death is not the biggest fear we have; our biggest fear is taking the risk to be alive – the risk to be alive and express what we really are." ~ Don Miguel Ruiz

It sounds like a movie . . . I gave my 45 page transfer report to the SAC on May 2, 2001, he denied it on May 21 and I told him I would need to take further action. Nine days later I was nearly killed in a car wreck.

It happened about four city blocks from the FBI office. A man was distracted on his cell phone and ran a solid red light at approximately 40 miles per hour. His white F-150 truck t-boned the passenger side of my car slamming my side into two cars. My car was then launched across an intersection and hit a pole head on.

I remember seeing a flash of his white truck just before he hit me and I came to for an instant before hitting the pole. I later learned that I had a concussion from my head hitting the door jam which knocked me unconscious. In the moments before I was extracted from the car, thoughts came that this was the end - I was about to die - and I had a peace about it.

A police officer I'll call Joe actually saw the accident and it turns out that he was my neighbor's friend and we knew one another. I could hear him yelling at me to turn the car off but my body wouldn't move, I couldn't see nor catch my breath. The airbag had deployed when the car hit the pole and I was breathing noxious gasses just before I passed out again. My next memory was realizing I was strapped to a board and feeling the movement of being carried. I reached up with my right hand and took hold of a very muscular arm. I couldn't

102

see the man it belonged to but I knew he was strong and felt I would be okay as long as I held on to him.

I was beginning to breathe better but still couldn't see – it was a very frightening experience – and then I realized I didn't know where my gun was. I started yelling "get my gun – get my gun" which put the paramedics in a panic. When I could finally think clearly enough to form a sentence, I told them I was with the FBI and there were weapons in the car. The FBI was called and soon agents were on scene. I also heard the paramedics say that they don't normally pull people alive from those kinds of accidents. If I hadn't been in such good physical shape, I would most likely have been killed.

My next memory is a very kind doctor leaning over me in the hospital explaining what had happened and where I was. He asked if I needed anything for pain. I remembered how sore I was throughout training at Quantico and was sure I'd be sore from a car accident so I asked for Motrin. I had no idea how injured my body was and I can tell you from experience that there was no pain in the first hours after the accident. That has actually brought me comfort - to know that if I had died that day I would not have been in pain. He also asked if he should contact my family. I said absolutely not. My parents would be frantic if called in another state and unable to talk with me.

There is no way the doctor could know what was going on and he felt he was doing the right thing when he let two agents come in to see me. One was my inept, irrational supervisor and the other was one of the "bad guys" since the OPR. It took everything I had not to scream for them to get out. Once I was taken to another area for an MRI I told the nurse how upsetting it was to have them there . . . they were neither family nor friends. I felt more comforted by complete strangers than by those people from the office. They were immediately asked to leave.

I was also clear headed enough to start worrying about the copy of my transfer report under the backseat floor mat of my car. It would stir up a hornets nest if agents were to find that. Joe came by to check on me and I asked him to get the report and hold it in confidence. He did one better . . . he actually took the time to get the report and bring it to me in the hospital.

After several hours and lots of tests, poking and prodding (and lying on shards of glass imbedded in my back) the doctor asked if he could offer something a little stronger for pain. By that time I said only one word, "Morphine!"

By the grace of God, I had no internal organ damage or broken bones. However, since I was hit in three different directions, I had severe organ bruising and soft tissue damage from my neck down to my tailbone. I also had a huge knot on my shin where my leg was rammed into the dashboard panel and the seat belt probably saved my life but it felt like I was almost cut in half. The hospital staff called Donna, my close friend from the office (non-agent) when I was released to go home and we went by to see the car - completely totaled.

After getting settled at home with ice packs, heating pads and a lot of Vicodin, muscle relaxers and Motrin (800mg), I pulled myself together enough to call my parents. I told them I had good news and bad news. They wanted the good news first so I told them I could finally get a Toyota 4-Runner – the vehicle I always wanted . . . then I explained what happened.

That was on a Wednesday and I was sure I'd be back at work by the following Monday so I pressed to get a rental car over the weekend. For the next four and a half months, that car never left my garage. During the first three days I felt like I was going to be alright. From day four through day twelve, the injuries became apparent and I felt excruciating pain throughout my body. The car wreck also triggered the onset of migraine headaches that I would battle for years to come.

When my doctor examined me, she said I would be off work for at least two weeks. That same news continued at each follow-up appointment. I didn't know why I wasn't just told from the beginning that it would take four and a half months before I could even think about going back to work. The doctor explained that there was no way I would've been able to emotionally accept that news. By giving me only weeks to think about, I could maintain the hope of recovery. I was put through numerous therapies to include Atlas Orthogonal and Myofascial Release.

Shelby, Donna and Elaine proved to be my angels on this earth. It was difficult for me to ask for help. Shelby didn't wait for an invitation. She saw what I needed and worked with my other friends to get things done. She mowed my lawn, cleaned my house, did laundry, changed my sheets and I later learned that she actually hid the car keys, counted my medication to be sure I was taking it correctly and was talking to my mother regularly giving her "care giver" updates on my recovery.

My friends brought me groceries, medications, took me to doctor and therapy appointments and Donna checked on me almost every week-day, bringing my mail from the office and my P.O. Box (which also reminded me to pay bills). My Bunco friends put me on a rotating "meals-on-wheels" program for dinner each day with leftovers for lunch. One woman was a nurse with extensive knowledge of healing and recovery. She gave me massages at my home and was instrumental in helping me get through the emotional and physical pain of this accident.

Simply put, I was pathetic. I couldn't stand up straight, nor long enough to even cook a meal. Walking was extremely slow and painful. On the days I was able to shower, I sat on the floor of my bathroom with my arm propped on the commode to hold a blow dryer on my hair. By the time I was finished, I was exhausted and hurting. There were times I just sat and cried because of the pain and I often wondered if I would ever be the same again.

I was taking ten Vicodin a day (along with muscle relaxers) that knocked me out to the point that I would not wake up when my friends came over. When my eyes were open, I was told I provided a lot of entertainment . . . they never knew what I'd be talking about or if I'd make sense . . . but they got a good laugh.

As I began to improve, Shelby made sure to get me out of the house and back in a car. She gave me an hours notice to get ready for good medicine . . . Baskin-Robbins ice cream. I am so grateful that she knew the importance of getting me out to go somewhere other than to the doctor. It really helped lift my spirits.

Car shopping on heavy narcotics proved to be an interesting experience and American Toyota had the perfect 4-Runner for me. Of course I was too loopy to know that without Shelby's help. My doctors would not allow me to drive and I still couldn't walk well so Shelby took me to the dealership and drove slowly up and down each isle until I found something I liked. While I was wandering around . . . Shelby found a great deal – a Limited program vehicle with all the bells and whistles. In my dazed state I kept asking if leather seats were a good thing . . . if wood paneling was a good thing . . . if a sunroof was a good thing? She convinced me that it was all a "good thing" and I took it for a test drive in a school parking lot.

It wasn't so much "testing" as it was pure entertainment for Shelby and the salesman - who belly laughed as I flew over speed bumps and made hairpin turns . . . or so I thought. Actually . . . she later told me I was only going about five mph but thought I was on a ride at Six Flags. When it came time to work the deal, I only remember the salesman going to his "boss" one time - that awful haggling process. He quickly came back and I told him I didn't hear one curse word and he better start fighting for me or I'd kick his heinie. Shelby told him it would be a good idea to get to the best price right away. Shortly thereafter, the price dropped, I signed the papers and Shelby enjoyed driving my new 4-Runner over the next two months.

In time I was able to manage the pain with less medication and I could think more clearly - and worry more. I was in financial strain with hospital and medical bills and to top it off, my supervisor and the Albuquerque management never even called to see how I was. However, they did do everything possible to make sure I wouldn't get a pay check. It took Shelby contacting FBI HQ before my sick leave and leave donations were applied and I was a topic of conversation in the office with people saying I wasn't hurt – I was just faking my injuries. When I told my doctor what the FBI was doing (even after having written three medical notes to them) and knowing how much that upset me, I was told that stress, anxiety and pressure was counterproductive to my healing and I should have no further discussions with the office until I returned to work.

As I thought about all the pain and difficulties I had to go through, I realized that . . . this was certainly not what I had in mind, but God did answer my prayer.

The week before the car wreck, I was driving to work and I noticed how bright and beautiful the day was. Mind you, the sun shines more than 300 days a year in Albuquerque and it hit me that I hadn't even "seen" the sun in ages. I was living in a dark fog - without brightness and light. I was angry that God would allow all these difficulties in my life and I prayed that He would fix my situation or take me home to Him. I was tired of dealing with all of it. I was harassed for being a truthful hard worker . . . I needed the conflicts to stop and have some calm in my life.

I believe God used the car wreck to get me out of the FBI office until I could be transferred. I didn't have to quit and I didn't have to put up with any more harassment. He surrounded me with people that took care of me and loved me and though there was a lot of pain involved . . . He gave me rest. God answered my prayer. He had the perfect opportunity to take me home to Him and let me die in the car wreck - but He didn't. That was powerful evidence that God is not finished with me yet - He kept me on this earth to fulfill His plan for my life.

After the FBI Director reviewed my transfer report, I was given a choice of seven FBI Field Offices (Chicago, Detroit, Houston, Los Angeles, New York, San Francisco and San Juan). I selected Houston, had transfer orders in hand by mid-August and was told the orders were personally signed by FBI Director Thomas J. Pickard. God answered my prayer and fixed my situation. Elaine sacrificed time with her husband and kids, driving cross-country with me and Shelby flew in to meet the movers in Houston. Only with their help would the doctors allow me to move - with the restriction that I was not to lift anything over ten pounds. Again, friend angel wings were showing.

FBI HOUSTON

I had high hopes for Houston, one of the FBI's largest offices. I was assigned to the Joint Drug Intelligence Group for a short time . . . until one of the four ASACs read my medical limitations about not being in physical confrontations. I was then moved to the Administrative Squad, and assigned to the Investigation and Intelligence component for all Houston Command Post Operations. Over the next three years, I conducted more than 700 FBI interviews for background investigations on FBI applicants, White House staff, Presidential appointees requiring Senate confirmation and Presidential pardons. I thoroughly enjoyed interviewing the top echelon business, community and even government leaders in the Houston area and I had time for physical therapy to continue my healing process.

It is difficult to compare the Albuquerque and Houston offices because my responsibilities in Houston kept me out of the office on interviews. Just as my "outside" impression of the FBI had been positive, that's what I encountered in the course of my duties on the "outside." I mostly kept a low profile and exchanged only pleasantries with other employees.

I did see that "best kept secret" again in full operation. My first day in the Houston office was also my first full day back at work and my neck and back pain made it difficult to work even eight hours, much less ten hours per day. The Houston office had in-office rotating weekend agent duty so for months I would contact the agent scheduled for each Saturday and ask to work their shift. It was not uncommon to trade weekends but apparently I was the first to ask for extra duty. I would explain that I was recovering from a car wreck and needed to work additional time for my AUO. The routine response I got, "Don't you know how to use a pen? Just write down extra hours." I would thank them and ask again to work their shift. My offer was never declined and it gave me the opportunity to meet agent and support personnel from other squads.

The first time I saw the Houston SAC, he was wearing a little red cowboy hat, riding a pony, outside the Boy Scout Building. The next time I saw him was at the yearly drunk fest . . . code name: *Annual Law Enforcement Cook-off.* He kicked off the festivities by being the first to slobber on the bottom of an ice block doing alcohol shots. The ice block was suspended at a 45 degree angle with a groove melted down the center. Alcohol was poured down the chute to be lapped up, ice cold at the bottom . . . one person after another.

I took the approach in Houston that the less personal information I knew about my fellow agents - the better. I made appearances at office functions and only sporadically went to lunch with other agents. I didn't like being guarded but after my experiences in Albuquerque, I had a long way to go in trusting anyone associated with the FBI. In time I relaxed my guard and made some friends, both agent and non-agent.

FBI employees are required to notify the CDC of any legal proceedings so my first encounter with Curt, the Houston CDC, was about my deposition with attorneys for the car wreck. CDC Curt was a gruff, overweight man who was a topic of office discussion, especially when he gave firearms briefings. Agents openly stated that if you weren't drinking or sleeping with him, you'd have problems. There were no pleasantries with CDC Curt; the conversations were kept brief and strictly professional.

The car wreck case took time and was finally settled just before trial. It was some relief that the man's insurance had to pay their policy limit . . . unfortunately it was not enough to cover the cost of my medical bills and lost wages. When all was said and done, I had over $50,000 of debt. I was given advice to file bankruptcy since none of it was my "fault" – but then again, it also wasn't the fault of those that had provided services and were waiting for payment. I did a lot of praying and I knew God was taking care of me. I was grateful to be healthy enough to work and to be working at a job that paid well. It would take many years . . . but I resolved to pay it off.

One of the most difficult things about the car wreck is that I never heard from the man that changed my life in an instant. He may have been instructed not to talk to me while the "case" was on-going . . . but in my mind once it was over it was simple human decency to make contact. It took some time to get over the anger of his carelessness but once I remembered that <u>everything</u> is filtered through God's hand – I was able to forgive.

 educativeeducativeeducative

"Do the right thing. It will gratify some people and as-tonish the rest." ~ Mark Twain

❧ *8* ❧

Coming Alive

The POWER of the Resurrection
Always Follows
The Suffering of the Cross!!!
✟

❧❧❧❧❧❧❧

A friend and former female FBI SA experienced gross mistreatment from the FBI. She was falsely accused of wrongdoing and then dismissed after 23 years of service. Even in her hardship, she encouraged me by sending Joel Osteen's book, ***Living Your Best Life Now,*** for Christmas. Joel is the pastor of Lakewood Church in Houston, Texas and as I read his book each night I could feel my spirit coming alive.

Natalie had suggested I find out about Lakewood and I'd tried to watch Joel several times on TV. However, I didn't think a guy that smiles so much could be genuine, much less trusted. Well, here's a news flash . . . when I turned down the volume and just watched him, I noticed the shape of his mouth. Even when he's not "smiling" – his teeth are showing, giving the appearance of a smile. There's no way I could fault a man for being just the way God made him.

I had been visiting various churches in the area but hadn't found one that felt like "home." I e-mailed several churches asking about their Single Adult Ministries and Lakewood was the only one to respond. Also, as a night owl, I was very interested in attending a church with a Saturday night service.

On January 15, 2005 I went to Lakewood for the first time and was absolutely blown away. After years of being the tough FBI agent in front of people and suffering through eight years of a spiritual desert, my heart opened and tears flowed freely. Once they started, they continued. First, when the choir sang. I wanted to find a church that was traditional – but alive! The choir was wearing beautiful blue and white robes, swaying to the music and "rockin' out." They were incredible!

More tears flowed with the overwhelming peace that I was in the right place. I felt God saying, "You've been seeking Me and here I am." Then I cried through Communion. I had not been to a church that served Communion in years and I melted with that tender, intimate time with the Lord. I felt I was exactly where I was supposed to be, doing exactly what I was supposed to do – it was incredibly powerful!

Joel's sermon was about working professionally in the area where God gifted you. That nearly knocked me out of my seat. Was I doing what God wanted by staying in the FBI? Tears streamed down my face because the answer was clear . . . no. I had worked hard and done a good job throughout my career but the FBI never fully utilized my gifts and talents . . . and when I did outstanding work I didn't receive recognition, I was told to slow down so I wouldn't make anyone else look bad.

A woman I met earlier in the evening assured me that God was directing my steps and He would put me right where He wanted me to be. I just needed to stay faithful and trust Him. I had a heavy heart as I walked to my truck. When I started the engine – the Steve Green CD began playing and I sat in the dark and wept as I listened to the song - ***He Who Began a Good Work*** - straight from scripture:

> *Being confident of this, that He who began a good work in you will carry it on to completion until the day of Christ Jesus.*
> *Philippians 1:6 (NIV)*

TEARS

I want to take a moment to mention tears. As an FBI SA, it was not acceptable to have a tender heart, to care, to be affected by horrendous sights . . . dead bodies covered with maggots, a grandmother shot through the eye, a woman raped by a uniformed police officer during a traffic stop, children and adults kidnapped and abused, etc.

My job was to be unemotional and "handle it" – and I did – but here's the thing . . . I understand that I had a job to do and needed to be strong. However, it's not wrong to have a heart, to feel something, it's not wrong to talk (in a safe environment) about difficult things that happened and it's not wrong to cry. It is unbelievable to me that not one supervisor ever asked me if I was okay after dealing with difficult cases. FBI agents are made into robots. The unspoken policy to "Suck it up and be tough - just handle it!" needs to be addressed. Unfortunately, I was slowly turning into one of those cold, hard FBI robots.

In the year that I've been away from the FBI, God has restored my heart and revived my compassion for others . . . and He has allowed me to "feel" again, the good, bad and awful. He has also placed incredible family members and friends around me to guide me through this transition . . . to being a healthy Christian woman.

Below is a sampling of scripture references about tears mostly describing the crying out **by men**. Far from being a sign of weakness, it is a deep human quality and gift we are given to release pain and grief (opening the heart for healing), or an expression of overpowering goodness and joy. (For a complete understanding, I encourage you to do a personal study on 'tears,' 'weeping' and 'wailing').

> *You keep track of all my sorrows. You have collected all my tears in your bottle. You have recorded each one in your book? Psalm 56:8 (NLT)*

> *He will swallow up death forever. The Sovereign LORD will wipe away the tears from all faces; he will remove the disgrace of his people from all the earth. The LORD has spoken. Isaiah 25:8 (NIV)*

> *Those who sow in tears will reap with songs of joy. Psalm 126:5 (NIV)*

> *I am worn out from groaning; all night long I flood my bed with weeping and drench my couch with tears. Psalm 6:6 (NIV)*

For you, O LORD, have delivered my soul from death, my eyes from tears, my feet from stumbling. Psalm 116:8 (NIV)

Then he threw his arms around his brother Benjamin and wept, and Benjamin embraced him, weeping. Genesis 45:14 (NIV)

He turned away from them and began to weep, but then turned back and spoke to them again. He had Simeon taken from them and bound before their eyes. Genesis 42:24 (NIV)

For his anger lasts only a moment, but his favor lasts a lifetime; weeping may remain for a night, but rejoicing comes in the morning. Psalm 30:5 (NIV)

I was getting more and more excited about the activities at Lakewood, but at that time I was going to work, coming home, taking a nap, cooking dinner, watching TV and going to bed. I didn't have a very exciting life and honestly . . . I wondered if I had the energy to do anything other than work.

In early February I auditioned for the Lakewood Players Drama Team. I had a great time and it felt good (and different) to let loose a little. I even used my New York accent in one sketch and from what I was later told - - - got the highest marks on my audition. However, I wasn't asked to join the team, I was asked to help with KidsLife.

This didn't make sense to me. I had been a professional actress but wasn't "good enough" to make a church drama team? And God knew how much I wanted to be married and have children. Rather than blessing me with kids, He was asking me to work with other peoples kids and be around married couples. Somehow it just didn't seem fair.

I checked my attitude and remembered that serving God is doing what He asks me to do . . . where He asks me to do it. I began to plan, coordinate and direct drama workshops, and you know what? It was fantastic! The kids, and the leaders, were great. I found the joy in acting and having fun again - and I found myself laughing. It had been such a long time since I really laughed. It touched me deeply when kids threw their arms around me saying, "You Rock, Miss Tracy!"

*Let us not become weary in doing good, for at the proper time
we will reap a harvest if we do not give up.
Galatians 6:9 (NIV)*

*A joyful heart is good medicine, But a broken spirit dries up
the bones. Proverbs 17:22 (NASB)*

Six months after my audition, I was asked to be on the Lakewood
Player's team. Because I worked well with KidsLife, I continued
helping and soon found myself blessed to be involved with nearly
every ministry in the church . . . and quickly became director and pro-
ducer for numerous church events. One month later I was asked to
teach a Single Adult Bible Study . . . and I found that I wasn't tired
any more. I was becoming more energized by doing God's work.

As I continued serving at Lakewood, I thought there must be a bug
in my house. Joel's messages spoke directly to me and my situation.
It was amazing how in-sync his sermons were with what I needed to
hear at that particular time. I kept a journal of each service for an entire year so I could go back and look up scripture and remember his
key points. It was definitely God's hand that placed me at Lakewood
Church.

I also realized that I had a lot of "junk" in me, specifically anger in
dealing with the way I had been treated in the FBI. I couldn't do anything about what had happened. I had to learn how to forgive, move
forward and find a way to be thankful, even grateful. An ungrateful
life where expectations are not met is filled with frustration and discontent. Gratefulness is the fuel that produces a happy life. I had a
long way to go and the only one that could help me was God.

*Enter His gates with thanksgiving and His courts with praise;
give thanks to Him and praise His name. Psalm 100:4 (NIV)*

I began to understand what the "sacrifice of praise" means. There
were a lot of times I just didn't feel like "praising." I looked forward
to going to church, but when I got there, I was often tired, cranky, angry - just fill in the blank. I quickly found that if I would lay all that
down before God and make a small effort, He would take the "junk"
away and fill me with His strength and joy.

Coming Alive

The LORD is my strength and my shield; my heart trusts in him, and I am helped. My heart leaps for joy and I will give thanks to him in song. Psalm 28:7 (NIV)

In April of 2005, I felt things moving in my life, an uneasiness and excitement that things were changing for the better. Joel spoke about the "pain of change." But if you are obedient to God, you won't be able to outrun the good things God has for you. It's important to pay attention and be sensitive when God is moving on your heart. It's also important to open yourself to hearing what God is saying. I didn't know what was coming, but I knew it would be great! It was also scary to think about change and this is where I made some mistakes.

I got very "busy" doing God's work; busy going to church, busy working in ministry and busy with activities. I also found that I did a lot more talking to people about God than talking to God. Maybe I was afraid of what I'd hear. I know that fear is not of the Lord. There are 365 "fear not's" in the Bible . . . that's one for every day! It would have served me well to learn that lesson here, but I'll tell you more about that later.

I also went through a "Healthy Soul Seminar" by Leo Tyler - (www.HealthySoul.org). I thought it would be a good exercise but didn't think I'd get much out of it. I was so wrong. Leo has an amazing way of communicating the love God has for us . . . and how we can hinder our relationship with Him by holding on to the wrong things. We have everything we need to conquer evil and there's no sense in dragging bad "stuff" around with us. That's like carrying a trash can on your back.

God can handle all my problems and I realized *I was the problem* when I wouldn't give everything to Him. I was destroying myself by holding on to bad things, and there is no way I could move closer to God unless I was obedient to forgive others and let go.

I had a light bulb moment when I realized I was *TIRED* of being angry. I was downright mad at what I had been put through. I had a list of evil people that had hurt me, been instrumental in snuffing out God's light in me, and seemed to take great pleasure in spreading poison everywhere they went. I couldn't hold on to that any more. I was exhausted . . . and I knew my future depended on letting go - of everything.

As I thought of each person on my bad guy list – I got that sick knot in my stomach that churns up a fire. I had three choices: 1) keep

115

thinking about everything each person had done, feeding and stoking the anger, 2) ignore addressing any problem and stay where I was, or 3) give them over to God. It may seem like an easy answer, but even bad things, given enough time, become comfortable. Think of bad "loving" relationships, bad habits, negative thinking. Making a choice to do something differently doesn't feel "normal" or "right" at first.

After some struggle, I did give each person over and asked that God would help me to forgive and let go of all the anger, hatred and negative thoughts I still had toward them for what they did. Holding on to all that would be like drinking poison and hoping they got sick.

Forgiveness is not excusing what was done to me, or saying it was okay. Absolutely not! Forgiveness is recognizing that what these people had done was pure evil. They were willing participants used by Satan for his evil. Evil and lies always come from the pit of hell. Forgiveness is turning all those hateful, negative, hurt feelings over to God for Him to handle. Forgiveness released me from that festering hatred that was killing me from the inside out.

I had to get to the point of realizing that no sin is greater than another. We, as humans, often categorize sin. We think that murder is #1, and there's a pecking order down to . . . maybe taking the Lord's name in vain as #38 and gossip being #70 or so. That is not true in God's eyes. All sin is the same to God. Each sin is equal. It's hard to wrap the mind around the perfection, love and goodness of God. Think of it in terms of black and white (no gray areas). Any sin we commit, ANY – is like a black cloth that covers us . . . it doesn't matter how small it is, kinda like being pregnant . . . either you are or you're not. You can't be a "little" pregnant, just like you can't commit a "little" sin. God, in His perfection, cannot look at sin. Even on the cross, when Jesus took on all the sins of the world, God loved His Son, but He had to look away from the sin on Him.

> *And at the ninth hour Jesus cried out in a loud voice, "Eloi, Eloi, lama sabachthani?"—which means, "My God, my God, why have you forsaken me?" Mark 15:34 (NIV)*

I used to think that was such a horrible thing for God to do to His Son . . . but it was the ultimate act of love for us. Jesus took on the sins of the world. He died, He went to hell, and He overcame hell to go home to be with God, His Father. How can Jesus know what I go through? How I feel? He knows because He took on *EVERYTHING* while He was dying on the cross.

I know I can live with Jesus' grace and covering. When I pray to God, through His Son, Jesus - the black cover of sin is removed and God sees only His perfect Son. Then He hears me.

I've had people make fun of my positive outlook on life and I've been told that I see through rose colored glasses. That's true . . . because I try to see through the filter of Jesus. I see that my rose colored glasses are really blood covered glasses. What a comfort to know that's how God sees me . . . through the blood covered glasses of His Son, Jesus.

When I accepted that the horrible things people did to me were no worse than any sin I ever committed . . . I knew I had to get clean with God and let Him take care of my situation, my humiliation and my hurts. Once I let go of all that junk - I felt the weight of the world lift off my shoulders and I knew I could rest in Him.

> *Come to me, all you who are weary and burdened, and I will give you rest. Matthew 11:28 (NIV)*

I had great peace that my enemies, those evil people that hurt me - a child of the most high God, would have to answer to Him for what they had done. When I came to Houston, I remember thinking that the best in my life was behind me - back to the years before I ever thought about being in the FBI. Now I could see that the best was still to come.

> *But the path of the [uncompromisingly] just and righteous is like the light of dawn, that shines more and more (brighter and clearer) until [it reaches its full strength and glory in] the perfect day [to be prepared]. Proverbs 4:18 (AMP)*

If you've ever heard Joel Osteen at Lakewood Church, he often encourages people to "Give us a year of your life and you'll never be the same." That was definitely true in my case. When I started going to Lakewood in January 2005, I had a career as a Special Agent of the FBI. One year later I was being stripped of my badge and gun and escorted out the door.

"Hear Me, you who know what is right, you people who have My law in your hearts: Do not fear the reproach of men or be terrified by their insults. For the moth will eat them up like a garment; the worm will devour them like wool. But My righteousness will last forever, My salvation through all generations." Isaiah 51:7-8 (NIV)

❧❧❧❧❧❧

"Sir, my concern is not whether God is on our side; my greatest concern is to be on God's side, for God is always right." ~ Abraham Lincoln

๛ 9 ๛

Facing the Lifeless Eyes of Rage

"You gain strength, courage, and confidence by every experience in which you really stop to look fear in the face. You must do the thing which you think you cannot do." ~ Eleanor Roosevelt

๛๛๛๛๛๛

When I was offered the position as Intern Program Coordinator (IPC) for the FBI Houston office, I was well aware that no one else wanted the job. The previous IPC retired as a crusty, bitter old man who took pleasure in "barking" at the college interns whom he selected. Stories circulated and agents laughed about his negative behavior toward the students, having been heard to often respond to them, "What the **** do you want?" I was not impressed with his demeanor and thought it extremely sad that a senior FBI SA got his kicks by bullying college students. He was regarded as a complete jerk. The student interns were given the privilege to work (without a paycheck) within the FBI office for a college semester to receive academic credits and a big star on their resume. In no way did their volunteer status reduce them to the level of being his personal whipping posts.

Once named as the IPC, I received all the previous files . . . which consisted of one banker-size box half filled with loose coffee stained documents. Apparently, the IPC some eight years prior initiated the program without implementing FBI HQ requirements. By the time the "crusty" IPC came on board, he didn't have time for FBI rules, much less documentation. The previous interns had no contracts in place between the FBI and their universities, no documented authorization to be working within FBI space and no files reflecting their performance. In fact, FBI HQ didn't know there were interns working in Houston.

Though not employees, with proper documentation the interns would receive workers compensation if injured. There was not even a list of names to verify if an intern had ever worked at the FBI. I created the intern program essentially from scratch.

Education and helping young people set their feet on firm foundation has always been important to me. I was part of the FBI Speakers Bureau from the time I entered on duty and was consistently called on to speak to schools and community groups. As the IPC, I was excited to be in a position to assist college students in providing a unique and productive experience, all while benefiting the FBI with "a free labor workforce." I also knew I'd need a lot of legal assistance to develop the intern guidelines from a liability standpoint. I worked hand-in-hand with the Acting Assistant Special Agent in Charge (A/ASAC Ron) – acting meaning he was a supervisor filling in a vacancy, and with CDC Curt. CDC Curt instructed me to work with his assistant, ADC Keith, because CDC Curt didn't want to deal with "those interns."

When I spoke to ADC Keith about us working together and asking for his guidance about legal matters, he commended me on developing the program and stated, "You don't want an OPR."

Anyone can make an allegation against a fellow employee (even anonymously) with or without any evidence or substantiation. OPR's can take from one to three years to investigate (sometimes longer) and generally employees cannot be transferred or promoted while under investigation. Interestingly, there are many cases when employees make allegations just to "mess" with someone and there are no repercussions for individuals that make those false allegations. The OPR system is seriously flawed. FBI Director Mueller commissioned a study of OPR by Attorney General Griffin Bell and Dr. Lee Colwell. Their 2004 report is located at the computer link provided, with some excerpts below:

> ♦ *OPR as an operating entity has lost touch with its original mission and no longer effectively serves the Director and the FBI as a whole. OPR has become an unfortunate lightning rod both outside and within the Bureau as a perceived source of unfairness and favoritism*

♦ *Of great concern is that OPR has become so stigmatized that it is extremely difficult to attract top personnel to sensitive OPR positions requiring the highest levels of experience, judgment, and discretion.*

♦ *The FBI should develop and uniformly apply effective "punishment guidelines."*

♦ *The "bright line" policy of termination for cases of "lying, cheating and stealing" has become blurred and no longer serves its original purpose. The resulting confusion over the standard also is viewed by some as allowing leniency for SES employees* [FBI Upper Management].

♦ *The background and experience of the adjudicators is highly variable and leads some to conclude that the OPR process is a "crap shoot," depending on which adjudicator is assigned.*

♦ *Recommended improvements relating to . . . protection against unfounded allegations of misconduct and selective prosecution of cases.*
                    www.fbi.gov/publications/opr/bellreport.pdf

I didn't give ADC Keith's comment about OPR much attention at the time but in hindsight, perhaps he knew about things brewing, things building against me as I walked forward completely unaware.

The intern program was a collateral (or side) duty. However, because it was in such shambles, I gave up my personal life and worked tirelessly to develop it to be an exceptional program indicative of the FBI I was proud to serve and partner to the public educational community as well as each individual intern. I worked my full-time responsibilities and then dedicated an exorbitant amount of time to develop the intern program. Though I worked through too many nights and weekends to count, I felt that helping college students was more than worth my sacrifice and I knew once the program was fully developed and functioning . . . maintaining the program would be a breeze.

Through exhaustive efforts, I developed all the elements necessary to provide the Bureau with a sound intern program that included all FBI HQ criteria, an objective selection process as well as intern work assessment and evaluation. I created an Intern Program Coordinator Notebook (approved by the Houston A/ASAC, ADC and FBI HQ personnel), and created an Intern Notebook (again with all approvals) filled with orientation and other information students would need for a solid foundation when entering the FBI.

I also ensured that the interns were exposed to many different facets of the FBI and other law enforcement components. I worked with countless agents and other professionals to allow the interns to interact with various squads performing different missions and tasks, observe command post operations, ride with surveillance groups, have group meetings with high level FBI management and federal judges, tour a prison, watch an autopsy, shoot at the FBI firearms range and learn about training techniques, participate in SWAT and ERT training exercises, accompany Houston Police Department helicopter pilots in aerial surveillance instruction, as well as many other activities. Their experiences were educational, very valuable and . . . they had a great time! This also gave FBI personnel an opportunity to meet, interact with and evaluate prospective employees, support and agent, who might join the FBI in the future. Previous interns primarily shadowed one agent and did grunt work. None had ever been given the access and experiences they received under my supervision.

At the end of each semester, I received numerous cards and notes from the interns with expressions of gratitude for my hard work in making so many opportunities available to them . . .

♦ "It surpassed my greatest expectations. I learned more in that semester than all my others combined. And it definitely confirmed my career path in federal law enforcement."

♦ "Thank you for your tireless dedication to safeguarding not only our safety, but also our experience. I know that my future plans have greatly been shaped by this summer and I have you to thank."

♦ "The internship is a wonderful and memorable experience that I will never forget. I could not have wished for anything better. I appreciate all that you have done for not only me, but the group of interns as a whole."

♦ "I just wanted to give you a small thank you note to let you know how much I appreciate the time and effort you've put into this internship experience. Without a doubt, my time here would not have been as exciting and rewarding if your efforts on our behalf weren't always a priority. Thank you very much."

♦ "Congratulations on being the best intern coordinator of all time!"

♦ "Just wanted to thank you for everything you have done for me. I know you worked really hard for us. I will never forget the summer of '04. Take care of yourself and I hope to join you and the FBI in the near future."

♦ "I wanted to tell you how much I appreciate you being the Internship Coordinator. This internship has been so much better than I ever imagined it to be because of what you have done for the program and people involved. I can tell your heart is truly in the right place. It has been a privilege to get to know you and I will remember this experience for a lifetime."

Having a Public Relations/Marketing background was helpful for publicizing the program and developing marketing materials to include a brochure and executive presentation. I worked with the IT guru to create an intern program presence on the FBI website and made it a point to photograph as many activities as possible and provide each intern with a copy of their semester photographs. I also arranged for each intern to participate in a final presentation to FBI and university personnel which allowed the opportunity for public speaking experience, college credit that substituted for a final exam paper and an audience so the FBI SAC could present the interns with a certificate of appreciation from the FBI Director as well as a beautiful FBI glass plaque. My efforts were rewarded only in the satisfaction that each student had an exceptional experience.

The intern program was extremely successful and received local attention from FBI and community personnel, surrounding universities, and the Houston FBI management who sent me to San Antonio to brief their division and universities to duplicate the program. I also received recognition from FBI HQ and was notified that I supervised more interns than all the other FBI divisions combined. They also designated my program as the model for all Intern Programs throughout the FBI's 56 field divisions nationwide.

The success as the IPC and in performing all my "real" duties as an SA, equated to some very unhappy people . . . particularly CDC Curt it seems. There's a ridiculous, but accurate saying in the FBI, "If you're happy and successful, you will be reassigned until you're not." I still had an EEO lawsuit pending (detailed in Chapter 10 – *Battling FBI Lies*) and I was not only successful, but very much enjoyed each area of my responsibilities. I should've known there was a tornado coming.

In the summer of 2004, the new intern group arrived . . . thirteen (13) of them. Interns had to be selected six to eight months prior to their arrival so their background process could be completed. It seems that the old "crusty" IPC's last act was to accept every student that applied for the summer semester. He knew he wouldn't have to supervise them so he made it as difficult as possible for whoever came after him . . . it just happened to be me. Most semesters had three to five interns yet I was expected to single-handedly run the program alone. I requested much needed assistance through A/ASAC Ron, which was denied - so I just worked harder and got the job done.

As the IPC, I assigned each intern a "Direct Report," an agent they would work with throughout the semester any time they were not participating in group intern activities or on special assignments. This provided continuity and a "home base" to each intern with their own desk area, computer and phone extension.

Some of the interns were outstanding in their attitude, commitment, and respect for the FBI. Others made me fully understand what I've often heard about the "younger generation's lack of work ethic and their arrogant attitudes of entitlement."

One intern actually yelled at me because he had been asked to help shred the documents of an outgoing ASAC. He informed me that he was a professional and well above "those" tasks. I let him throw his temper tantrum and get it out of his system. He adamantly stated that he would not tolerate being treated like a secretary. Once he finished his ramblings, I explained that all agents are expected to write their own reports, make copies, shred their own documents or do *anything* necessary to get the job done. I also addressed his "position" and asked where he saw himself in the pecking order of the FBI. As he identified each position from the SAC all the way down to what he perceived as the lowest position (putting himself somewhere in the middle) . . . I reminded him that everyone he mentioned was an actual FBI employee and received an FBI paycheck - everyone that is, except him. His stance relaxed, he laughed a little and said he'd go back and shred documents.

Some interns showed only isolated incidents of inappropriate be-havior (like the one described above), somewhat expected of young college students taking their first steps into the real-world. Unfortu-nately, others were immature, at times disrespectful, not mindful of authority, and even disregarded FBI policies and rules enacted in part for their own safety. They demonstrated much less than what you would expect from college age students granted the unique opportunity to intern at the FBI. There were incidents of inappropriate racial comments, interns feeling they were mistreated by squad members and coming to me in tears, driving an FBI vehicle (a major liability no-no), and misuse of Bureau resources (in one case an intern used the FBI photo lab - intended for official FBI cases and crime photos - to de-velop over 100 personal family, baby and graduation photographs). As the IPC, it was my responsibility to resolve these issues and main-tain a professional and well run program.

For example, all the interns were told at orientation and agreed to in writing, that they would not participate or accompany SAs on arrest operations. This was a no brainer! "FBI Intern Shot in 'SAFE' Ar-rest" was not the headline we were looking for. I also told each of the interns that they were responsible for their actions. Regardless of what others might do, they were to hold themselves to the standard of doing the right thing.

Of course, not all SAs have their brains engaged and thought it would be fun to impress their interns and take them along for "cool arrest operations." Even *after being told not to do so,* interns went along and even invited other interns to participate. They also made sure to tell everyone not to let me know (so they wouldn't get in trou-ble). Imagine my surprise when I got a phone call from CDC Curt (the one that didn't want to deal with 'those interns') screaming at me, "Tracy, what the **** are your interns doing!!!" When it was discovered that agents had disregarded policy and taken interns on arrests, CDC Curt simply sent out an e-mail reminding everyone in the division that it was not to happen again. By the way, those agents were never reprimanded for their poor judgment and violation of FBI policies.

Even a supervisor that put an intern in a precarious position, jumping out of an FBI car in the middle of a downtown street yelling back for the intern to drive, was never reprimanded by FBI management. In handling this situation, I understood the position the intern was placed in and he did what he felt was right in the moment – no problem. However, he tried to cover it up and told three fellow interns to deny it happened. Asking people to lie is not doing the right thing.

At the beginning of the summer semester, an intern whom I'll call Sam made it a point to tell me that his university internship coordinator (a very well respected professor) would not recommend him for the FBI internship and didn't want him to participate. That upset Sam so he went over the professor's authority to complain to the university dean who then called the Houston FBI SAC to get him into the FBI program. At the time I was not clear why he was telling me this. Was it just conversation or was he bragging about his powerful "connections?" I disregarded it as a previous personality conflict and assured Sam that I did everything possible for each intern to receive fair treatment in the FBI. Sam also tried to impress me by excessively talking about his previous service in the Marine Corp.

I invited the interns to stop by my office area any time they needed to ask a question or get information but I quickly noticed that Sam was stopping by on an almost daily basis (and sometimes several times a day) just to "talk." I was extremely busy with my case load and often excused myself from his conversations. It didn't take long to recognize that I had a professional "brown-noser" on my hands. I exchanged pleasantries with him and then directed him back to his assigned squad area.

Sam soon stood out as having a bad attitude toward the rules and administration of the intern program. He was also disrespectful toward distinguished individuals who took the time and effort to speak to the interns. During a meeting with a Magistrate Judge, Sam put his head down, covered his face and demonstrated bizarre behavior I had never seen before. He "picked" at himself . . . as if there were things all over his arms and legs. He also arrogantly slouched down in his chair and refused to pay attention. Knowing that everyone can have a bad day, I overlooked Sam's behavior on that particular day.

The intern group became more and more upset by Sam's behavior as the weeks went on. I received consistently negative comments about him: "he's ruining it for everyone," "what's wrong with him?" "He's weird;" . . . "strange;" . . . "creepy;" . . . and "bizarre."

When I observed Sam during a briefing by high level FBI management, he was slumped in his chair rocking vigorously and strangely moving his eyes and head. After the meeting I spoke with Sam privately about his behavior that day and when he was in front of the Judge. I stressed that it was an honor for the interns to have these high level officials speak to them; they deserve respect and to have Sam's full attention and his behavior would not be tolerated. I later received information that he continued his inappropriate behavior with NASA officials.

By this time, Sam was on my radar as being difficult and I noticed his behavior more and more. When the interns had the opportunity to fire a semi-automatic sub-machine pistol with the FBI firearms instructors, Sam bragged about his service with the Marine Corp and fired excessively in an aggressive manner, causing further negative intern comments.

The interns also participated in a prison tour. A female intern rode up to the prison in a car with Sam. She reported to me that she was so frightened of Sam that she would not get back in the same car for the return trip. She said "He's the kind of guy that would take an Uzi and mow people down."

The interns were required to provide weekly reports of their assignments. In an effort to further improve the intern program, I designated the bottom section of the report for "Wishes." There were no instructions or parameters given for what they could ask but I began to notice that while most of the other interns requested activities that would expose them to other areas of law enforcement (one exceptional intern consistently wished for ways to improve himself in learning and contributing during his internship), Sam made requests "to go paint balling with other interns," "for Tracy to throw all the interns a big party at her place before we go!!!" and "use the last Wednesday of the internship for all of us to go to Six Flags in Houston." Sam had no interest in contributing to the FBI; he wanted the FBI (specifically me) to make sure he got to do only what he wanted and to have a good time.

Because negative reports continued about Sam's attitude and demeanor, I spoke with Larry, his Direct Report and Joe, the squad supervisor where he was assigned. I was surprised to learn that both these men had very positive comments about Sam. It didn't even sound like the same person I had observed, nor the behavior other interns had witnessed.

I then got reports that Sam was not participating in the team project final presentation. Two of his teammates (females) were concerned that the team would be thought of poorly because of his actions. Rather than single him out, I met with all the interns and reiterated that the final presentation was a group project and every member was to make contributions. Despite several meetings, Sam refused to step up and do little more than make copies of computer disks.

Throughout the semester, interns wrote university reports that I reviewed and edited. Rather than give them the feel of a "teacher" with a red pen, I used a blue pen to make any corrections or comments. Interns made the changes identified and returned the edited and clean copy back to me for final review. Sam was fully aware of this process, yet when I revised his longest report due (16 pages) late in the semester, Sam shredded the edited version so I would have to review the entire paper again.

As the semester wore on, Sam became pushy with me and blatantly disregarded my authority. Sam's behavior took on a new dimension when I denied his request for a day off to throw a party for all the interns at his residence during working hours. I told him it sounded like fun and he could do anything he wanted but it could not be an "FBI Intern" function. I couldn't allow an FBI sponsored event without FBI personnel attending. Sam argued with me that he was the "intern spokesman" and they all really wanted this party. I told him to go ahead and have it but it wouldn't be through the FBI. I later learned that he was "self-appointed" and many interns were not aware of his request, nor would they attend his event. It turned out that he was trying to impress his girlfriend (another intern) for her birthday.

He continued to argue with me and I firmly said, "Sam, the answer is no." I witnessed a transformation I have never seen before. Sam deliberately drew in air through his nostrils and physically bowed up at me while his hands tightened into fists. His body became rigid and he started to shake. His eyes were cold and lifeless, his face turned red and his lips were clenched tightly together. He stood in my open office area not three feet from me with no barrier between us, glaring at me. He maintained that posture and didn't speak.

Being mad and being filled with rage are two completely different things. We all get mad when things don't go our way and I've seen plenty of *extremely* mad/angry people in my lifetime – especially during some arrests. Rage is different. Rage is an explosive anger that comes just before a violent outburst. I had only seen the face of rage one other time when I was in my early-twenties. That encounter led to me being thrown into a glass door and then choked over the back of a chair.

I was looking into that face of rage again. After long, intense moments, I tried to diffuse the situation by changing the tone of my voice. I said, "Okay, well if there's nothing more, I need to get back to work. I'll talk to you later." He continued to stand frozen in that position so I turned around to face my desk. I have to admit I was scared. As I turned toward my desk, I flinched not knowing if he would come after me. It was obvious that Sam harbored substantial animosity toward me but my greater concern was his unnatural overreaction. After this incident, I became aware that Sam was voicing his discontent by making negative and hateful comments about me to a number of people.

What I hoped was an isolated incident was not. As the semester neared its end, I was quite surprised to get a request from Sam to extend his internship. With the difficulties he caused throughout the semester and his rage toward me, he barely made it through the program. He certainly didn't deserve the privilege of an extension. However, I consulted his university professor and ADC Keith before making a decision. They both enthusiastically agreed with my decision. Unfortunately, I had to give Sam the news and I knew he'd be very upset . . . again.

I previously worked with an agent I'll call Dave and we spoke in the squad area outside the conference room just before I went to meet with Sam. He said it was not a good idea for me to meet with Sam alone and he offered to go with me. I was relieved and immediately took him up on his offer.

Sam was seated at the end of the conference table with Dave and me on either side of him. I told Sam that his extension request was denied and he would be out-processed the following day, as scheduled. With those words, Sam became enraged, similar to what I witnessed previously. He deliberately drew air through his nostrils and his face turned red with his eyes inflamed. He was looking around the room and squirming in his chair like a caged animal. Then he exclaimed in an intense and disrespectful tone that he would go [around me] to his squad supervisor, Joe. Dave immediately leaned his body across the table, hit the table hard with his open hand to startle Sam and raised his voice while forcefully saying, "This (pointing at me) - is your supervisor!" Dave's actions only escalated the situation and Sam was furious as Dave and I left the room. Dave commented that it sure didn't take Sam long to bow up at me. Dave was concerned for my safety so he escorted me away from Sam and to another building floor.

I was very shaken and disturbed by Sam's behavior and body language toward me. I normally didn't carry my gun in the office but because of my fear of Sam, I carried it with me in the office the following day. I felt very vulnerable and though I didn't want to overreact, I felt it necessary to be prepared to protect myself and others if necessary.

I asked Amy, an exceptional intern assigned to the same squad with Sam, about her observations over the semester. Sam openly discussed his disappointment with where I assigned him. Because of his "collegiate qualifications" and Marine experience, he felt he should've been assigned to work Counter-Terrorism, rather than Counter-Intelligence. He also manipulated agents and openly discussed his need to "get out of the office."

Most FBI computers were only set up for the FBI's internal network. One "open computer" per squad was available for use when needing Internet access. Sam spent an inordinate amount of time checking his personal e-mail and searching the Internet so FBI employees were unable to use the computer for official business. Sam also made comments that suggested he was getting "shafted" in some way so he spent, in her opinion, an excessive amount of time working on things other than FBI assignments. He also made it clear that he would not reach out to help others. He arrogantly told Amy that if they needed him, they could ask . . . they knew where to find him.

By Amy's account, Sam did not work well in group settings and he "intentionally rides the coat tails of others and willingly takes credit for the work he did not contribute to. This behavior exhibits his flaky mentality and unwillingness to work cooperatively with others." He also spent excessive time with his girlfriend in the squad area, to the point that agents were making negative comments about his behavior. Sam was condescending in his interaction with Amy and he expected squad members to pay for his lunch if they invited him along. According to Amy, Sam "exhibits an overbearing attitude of superiority and negative disposition."

This was very puzzling to me. How could she and other interns that worked directly with Sam have such a negative assessment of him while he continued to get good reviews from Larry and Joe? That question was only answered much later when it came to light that Larry had been transferred out of the squad area the second week after Sam's arrival. Larry was a former Marine (Semper Fi - faithful brother) so he and Sam decided not to tell me that Larry was not even in the same area with Sam. I was also told by numerous agents and interns (after Sam was gone) that Sam made it a point to "visit" with the squad supervisor, Joe, as much as possible . . . he was always in Joe's office laughing and cutting up. Apparently Joe had fallen for the "brown-noser" treatment I adamantly avoided. No wonder Larry and Joe's assessment of Sam was completely off-base with all the others. They never evaluated anything other than Sam's schmoozing ability.

Angry with my decision to deny his extension, Sam went on a mission to slander me and make derogatory statements to everyone he could find. He made complaints about me to his "buddy" Joe, my supervisor and to A/ASAC Ron. He even influenced other interns to tell A/ASAC Ron how "mean" I was. Apparently, he convinced these students that I had no right to tell them to comply with FBI and intern program rules. I was stifling their experience and I should've just looked the other way when each of them violated FBI regulations.

When I arrived in the office on Friday, without any discussion with me what-so-ever, my supervisor told me that I had made bad decisions about the interns, A/ASAC Ron reversed Sam's denial of extension, removed me as the IPC and I was not to do anything with the interns. I was shocked! I didn't know what was going on. I called A/ASAC Ron's office and was told he was not available. I then heard an overhead page that all the interns were to report to my supervisor's office for out-processing.

I had planned an end of semester pizza party for the interns and I told them to go and have a good time. Afterward, most of the interns came to my office area buzzing with questions. Even the interns Sam persuaded to complain about me were now in my area asking questions (I also received thank you cards and hugs from those complaining interns – even a card from Sam's girlfriend). They wanted to know why I wasn't at the party . . . Why I wasn't doing their final evaluation . . . Why I wasn't doing their out-processing . . . Why they were told I wasn't their supervisor any longer . . . Why my supervisor was being so condescending and saying negative things?! There was quite a commotion going on and all I could do was be professional and tell them to do as they were told.

I can never fully express how disappointed, hurt, angry and humiliated I was that day. The interns told me themselves what was said to A/ASAC Ron and that Sam was the ringleader. My feelings had little to do with what the interns said. They were just kids that saw me as the "bad guy" because I did my job and held them accountable to FBI regulations. They never thought about how much I did to give them freedom throughout the FBI. They felt that I stopped them from doing things they thought would be exciting. I addressed each issue with a professional, appropriate and discreet resolution within my authority as the IPC. I also took great care to ensure that each student's university grade and FBI standing was not adversely affected.

The sickness I felt was due entirely to the actions of A/ASAC Ron. I worked with him (and ADC Keith) hand-in-hand to create and implement THE intern program for the FBI. He had praised my work, my attitude and my professionalism for over eight months. Then, without the common courtesy of a phone call or discussion, he struck me down. It just didn't make sense.

A/ASAC Ron, ADC Keith and I finally met at the end of the day. A/ASAC Ron said the interns told him I was "mean" and a copy of the "Intern Acknowledgement" (the document each intern signed at orientation acknowledging they understood what was expected of them while working at the FBI) was placed on his desk with the signature blacked out. He was quite bewildered at why it was given to him since he, ADC Keith and I created and finalized the document. Apparently one of the interns thought A/ASAC Ron was unaware that the interns were being required to follow FBI rules.

ADC Keith said it was clear that Sam was the instigator and went to complain to A/ASAC Ron. Once he knew he had A/ASAC Ron's ear, he sent his girlfriend and a couple of others to ambush me by using A/ASAC Ron. I told A/ASAC Ron that his decision had cut me off at the knees. I was stunned that he would make such an important decision without any of the facts.

Through discussions with A/ASAC Ron over the following weekend, he understood the difficulties I faced with Sam throughout the semester. I reminded him that he told me to resolve any intern issues with ADC Keith. If problems arose that we could not resolve, we were to include him. ADC Keith was aware of what happened with Sam and had been consulted, as was the college professor, before Sam's extension was denied. To my thinking, there were no unresolved issues that needed A/ASAC Ron's attention. Obviously ADC Keith felt the same way.

A/ASAC Ron chastised me for not "throwing [Sam] out sooner." I explained that Sam continued to receive positive comments and reviews from Larry and Joe and I had to take their assessments into consideration. I felt my hands had been tied.

I read from two documents that I later provided to A/ASAC Ron: 1) expressing my disappointment in A/ASAC Ron's decision and asking for his support, and 2) my candid opinion of Sam:

> *It is apparent that Sam is extremely influential and persuasive. He presents himself as "polar opposite" depending on his need to impress, always mindful of his self serving goals. He is hurtful and dismissive toward individuals that he does not consider useful.*

> *My candid opinion of [Sam] based on observation and experience over the eleven week summer semester is that he is developmentally young, manipulative, immature, bossy, arrogant, unpredictable, disrespectful, deceitful, and the sole source for causing major dissension among the other interns and a number of FBI personnel. He has an enormous ego, cannot accept any correction and is vindictive when he does not get his way. Sam has continually demonstrated his negative impact caused by his poisonous nature.*

After our discussion, A/ASAC Ron was very angry and said he would not tolerate what had happened. He would personally make arrangements for Sam to be thrown out the following Monday. This made an interesting situation. Had Sam left when I proposed (just denying his extension) he would have a mediocre final evaluation (factoring Larry and Joe's very positive with my very negative assessment) but he would not have any derogatory information on his university or FBI record. Because A/ASAC Ron reversed my decision and approved his extension, Sam now had to be officially "removed" from the program. This caused him major problems with his university and the FBI.

Because Sam was the first intern in the history of the Houston program (74 students since 1995) to be dismissed, I drafted a letter under the SAC and A/ASACs signature. A/ASAC Ron told me to have ADC Keith review the letter for any legal issues and with ADC Keith's changes, the final version stated:

> *Sam did make contribution and met the requirements to complete the summer internship. A number of issues regarding him . . . and certain misrepresentations and consistent attitudinal problems - made it necessary to remove him from the Houston Division . . . and at this time, the FBI Houston Division will not be able to provide a positive reference for [him].*

This letter was addressed to Sam with his university dean and professor receiving a copy.

I saw Sam when I arrived at the office on Monday. He had been called in from riding with the surveillance team and was huddled against the wall talking with an agent from his squad. A/ASAC Ron was not in the office that day but he was true to his word and had made arrangements to have Sam booted out.

The next day, Tuesday, I met with A/ASAC Ron and gave him the computer disc and hard copy of the "Sam Letter" for his signature. A/ASAC Ron told me that he had gotten a call from the ASAC that had been traveling overseas (thereby opening the position filled by Ron) wanting to know what was going on with the interns. We were both more than a little perplexed by how the ASAC would have any knowledge about a local intern issue.

My "status" had not been officially discussed since Friday (when I was removed) and A/ASAC Ron told me that I was still the IPC. He tipped back in his chair and said he was looking forward to the new intern semester, he knew I was and in an annoyed tone said that as far as he was concerned, he didn't want to hear that kids [Sam's] name again. We both chuckled a little and because I had worked all weekend, A/ASAC Ron told me I could take Wednesday off to rest.

I reminded A/ASAC Ron that we still had interns scheduled to out-process in three days and because of all the confusion, I thought it best that my supervisor and I both work together on the out-processing to present a united front for the interns. He agreed that would be best for all concerned.

I also noticed that day that all my blue pens had been taken from my desk. I didn't like the government issued ink pens used by the FBI so for years I personally bought Pilot Easy Touch Medium blue pens in bulk. When I left on Friday I had about eight of them at my desk. I kept a lot of them because it was common for people to innocently walk away with one, but it was not common for them all to disappear in one day . . . in fact over my entire career that had never happened.

Late that night, I still could not figure out how an ASAC assigned overseas would know about a bad intern in Houston. Then it hit me that Sam had the ear of the ASACs wife, the agent I saw Sam talking to while huddled against the wall. She doesn't have the same last name as the ASAC and I didn't make the connection earlier. It made perfect sense that Sam had complained to the wife who passed on his sad story to her husband.

What's unusual is that Sam's influence was to the point that the wife involved her husband, who then took the action to call A/ASAC Ron. It still begs the question, "Why?" Now all the pieces of the puzzle fit and I felt the bow was tied around the entire matter.

Then the pens disappearing from my desk linked back to Sam. He hated that I corrected his papers and I'd heard that he made comments about "Tracy and her **** blue pen." It's amazing how many incidents and comments I had dismissed in passing.

I felt very calm as I relaxed and distanced myself to read all the documentation as a story. How had all of this happened? I still could not find a logical explanation for how influential Sam had been to so many high level personnel.

Then I used an old Army trick my dad taught me. He said when things get complicated and don't make sense . . . KISS it (Keep It Simple Stupid). I highlighted all the descriptors used for Sam throughout the documentation. When I got to the comments by Amy – it caught my attention that she had written three times, "get out." She was talking about Sam wanting to get out of the office but it made me start thinking about the outlets Sam had continually used.

Even from his first encounter with his professor, he found and used outlets for his anger when he didn't get his way. Sam continued with his influence and persuasion to manipulate his way around anyone that opposed him. Then I identified all the times he perceived me as his "bad guy" and I got *scared!*

When I went to bed that night I had fitful sleep. Each time I woke up I was covered in sweat and I had a terrible upset stomach. It wasn't like having the flu or food poisoning . . . I was in a state of fear. Each time I identified a situation that Sam got angry, he had found an outlet. Sam was even telling people that it was his decision to leave the FBI internship - because of personal reasons. Once he received the letter that boxed him in (no FBI recommendation which would undoubtedly result in discipline from his university) I was afraid his outlet would be aggression toward me (his perceived bad guy). I didn't want to be a coward but I couldn't deny Sam's negative behavior and actions toward me.

I finally called A/ASAC Ron Wednesday afternoon and told him, though he didn't want to hear about Sam, I had some serious concerns. He said if it had to do with safety we needed to talk. I told A/ASAC Ron about Sam's rage toward me on two occasions (luckily controlled at that point), he was aggressive with firearms and he influenced his girlfriend and a few other interns to go to a top FBI official and slander me . . . successfully. I reminded A/ASAC Ron that Sam had been extremely influential with his dean and numerous FBI personnel . . . to include him.

At that time, I had over 19 years of professional work experience, six and a half years working for TRW, a Government Contractor for Ballistic Missile Defense Systems where I was the Public/Customer Relations Specialist for clientele at the Pentagon in Washington, DC. I had been an FBI SA for more than seven years and yet this college student was so influential with A/ASAC Ron that he took the severe action of removing me from a position (where A/ASAC Ron had personal knowledge of my success) without even asking me a question for clarification. A/ASAC Ron's impression of Sam (the day he complained about me) was also in extreme contrast to those of us that had very negative experiences with him to include his professor and the majority of the intern group.

As I said before, I conducted over 700 FBI interviews for background investigations on FBI applicants, White House applicants, Presidential appointees and Presidential pardons. It is very unusual to get conflicting information about an individual unless there are serious (and explainable) reasons such as an ex-spouse, a disgruntled friend or co-worker, etc. Even in those cases, the majority of personal and character assessments are consistent. Sam is the only individual I have **_ever_** encountered that was evaluated, with polar opposite descriptors, by such a variety of personnel.

If Sam felt he was boxed in a corner (receiving the negative FBI letter) I had no idea how extreme his reaction would be toward me (his perceived bad guy). I knew that one person could negatively influence others, even to the point of Charlie Manson. I did not want that to be the case here. I tearfully expressed concern for my safety. A/ASAC Ron said he would hold the letter until we could meet. That evening I pondered facing the issue head on with FBI assistance.

A/ASAC Ron, ADC Keith and I met again on Thursday for further discussions. I told them that my "B" (in FBI, for bravery) had slipped the day before but it was back in tact. I suggested notifying Sam of the negative letter in person and having agents available to assist if necessary.

ADC Keith rolled his eyes and said that Sam was just a bad college kid. I told him Sam was in his early twenties. According to FBI information, most killers are between the ages of 18 to mid-20s. Sam had military experience, was more than capable of using firearms as he aggressively showed on the FBI range, and he was already angry with me - demonstrated through his actions. Sam could kill me just like an "adult" (I'm still not sure why ADC Keith was suggesting Sam's age disqualified him as a danger).

I told them about my study and research in psychology. I didn't want to be so right about Sam that I was killed, laying in a box in front of a church with everyone scratching their heads wondering why they hadn't seen the warning signs. I felt that the warning signs were all right there in the documentation. I asked for them to send the information to the "experts" – the FBI's BAU for review. It would be a win-win scenario. They would either verify my concerns or alleviate them and assure me there was no danger.

A/ASAC Ron said we could resolve this by not sending the letter at all. I didn't think the FBI should back down because I was afraid of Sam. Then A/ASAC Ron suggested only sending the letter to the university dean and professor. However, I wasn't sure if the dean had some sort of "relationship" with Sam. I reiterated that the professor never wanted, nor recommended Sam for the FBI intern program. It was the dean who reversed the professor's recommendation and contacted the FBI SAC to get Sam into the program. If Sam and the dean had a close relationship, Sam would likely see the letter through him.

A/ASAC Ron then said that we wouldn't send the letter at all. We would put a copy of the letter in the FBI file and I was to meet with the professor about the situation. The professor could decide if the dean should be notified. I felt that was a good resolution and it calmed me tremendously.

I spoke with my supervisor about working together to schedule a time to out-process the interns on Friday. I had an interview scheduled all morning but would be available in the mid to late afternoon. I was angrily told that I was not needed; the interns would be handled without me. Though I had full authority to stand as the IPC and argue the point that [the supervisor] was the one not needed . . . I went back to A/ASAC Ron and explained what had happened and about the supervisor's unwarranted anger toward me (a supervisor that had been poisoned by Sam). I felt the best resolution would be for both of us to out-process the interns. However, I understood that there had been a lot of confusion over the past week and if he wanted to keep the peace with the supervisor [since the interns were already told to go there] and have me start the new semester fresh, I would agree to that. I asked him to call me and let me know how he wanted Friday to be handled. I never got a call from him so I could only assume that he was avoiding all appearances of conflict and letting the supervisor out-process the interns.

I did, however, get a call from Claire, the Regional Employee Assistance Program (EAP) supervisor. She said that A/ASAC Ron had mentioned to her that I looked tired and he was genuinely concerned about me because of what had happened (what he did to me). He knew that I had not slept or eaten well since his decision on Friday. She said it was not required, but she was available if I'd like to talk. I told her about my interview the next day and if I didn't hear from A/ASAC Ron to assist with the interns, I'd stop by in the afternoon.

I interviewed Alex on Friday. He was a retired Navy pilot now working as the President and CEO of a space company. His office was about an hour and a half away from the FBI Houston office. He was a delightful man and I enjoyed talking to him about various topics. One of his stories really caught my attention. He said that when he was in his fighter jet and had to fly low and fast, he could not even glance to the side or he would lose his bearings and have to go up for altitude. He had to be absolutely focused with his eyes straight forward. That is actually a message in the Bible as well:

> *Keep vigilant watch over your heart; that's where life starts.*
> *Don't talk out of both sides of your mouth; avoid careless banter, white lies, and gossip. Keep your eyes straight ahead;*

ignore all sideshow distractions. Watch your step, and the
road will stretch out smooth before you. Look neither right nor
left; leave evil in the dust. Proverbs 4:23-27 (MSG)

I was thinking about that message as I drove back to the office.
Sam told lies and created distractions that had caused a lot of confusion and dust in the FBI. I needed to take to the higher ground. There
was no reason to press the issue that my supervisor was being unrea-
sonable. So what that I was the IPC and I should do the intern out-
processing? In the grand scheme of things it really didn't matter. I
needed to keep my eyes focused on meeting with Sam's professor and
moving on to the next semester.

When I got back to Houston, I went through the McDonald's drive-
through to get a salad (by the way, I lost 35 pounds by eating McDonald's chicken salads for lunch – Subway has Jared, McDonald's has
me). The girl at the window gave me a Hershey Kiss (now that's a
first in my life) and said, "Here's something sweet for when you're
finished." I believe that everything that happens to us is filtered
through God's hands. I wondered if her comment was about my lunch
or was about the entire situation I was going through.

Since I hadn't heard from A/ASAC Ron, I met with Claire as soon
as I got back to the office at about 3:30. We had a good conversation
and she told me she was a PhD and had a background working with
youth. I told her that I felt it was important to find someone to work
with me regarding the interns so they would not disrupt FBI operations
by showing up on the doorstep of the supervisors, ASACs or even the
SAC. It was imperative that the person identified would know what
was going on (without taking up all their time), and I suggested the
possibility of e-mail reports.

I told her that I asked for assistance with the intern program but
was still independently supervising all the interns. I could call on
ADC Keith with big issues (like denying an extension) and then go to
A/ASAC Ron if necessary - but I had resolved the day-to-day problems independently. Had A/ASAC Ron known about all the problems
Sam had caused throughout the semester, or the problems by every
intern that showed up at his door (or had he bothered to ask) he would
never have wasted his time talking to them when they showed up on
their last day at the FBI. I asked Claire if she might consider helping
me with the intern program as the "Ombudsman" and conduct the end

of semester intern surveys to help improve the program. Claire seemed excited about this suggestion and extended her offer to help if A/ASAC Ron agreed.

When I woke up on Saturday after my first truly restful night, I was still pondering Sam's influential, persuasive talent. This was the most bizarre professional situation I had ever gone through and it stemmed from one strange college student. Maybe if he'd just influenced his peer group it would never have caught my attention . . . but he influenced some very high level university and FBI personnel. I wanted to learn more - to know what makes people listen to someone that is so polar opposite. On one side having completely negative characteristics with a black cloud over them . . . and on the other being able to influence and impress. I wanted to know how to recognize and handle someone like this in the future.

I went to my computer and started searching the Internet for negatively influential people. The search didn't produce results for Robert Schuller, John F. Kennedy, Jr. or Anthony Robbins - men with solid character using their influential talents to help others. I found people like Charles Manson who used his talents to influence hippies with troubled lives to murder at his instruction. In fact, a lot of the information that came up was about killers. I thought it was a bit outlandish so I skimmed the information and went on. Then something I read reminded me of Ted Bundy. I remembered a television special on "Dark Heart, Iron Hand" that Bundy was an attorney and had represented himself at his trial.

I read some information about Bundy and couldn't help but notice things that seemed similar to what I had observed in Sam's behavior. I was looking for those particular things that make a person influential but kept being struck by all the similarities I was finding between Sam and Bundy. I thought it must just "seem like a lot" so I printed out the information and applied KISS (Keep It Simple Stupid). I highlighted things that were similar to Sam and I wrote in the margin what I had observed in Sam's actions and behavior. I know there can be very innocent similarities between all kinds of people and personalities that are purely coincidental. However, as I got to 10, then 20, then 30 - my concern was heightened.

When I was finished, my mouth was dry and I was terrified – I counted 47 similarities between Sam and Bundy. That just seemed too many to discard, especially since some were profoundly specific and peculiar, not what you would consider to be "normal."

I was very concerned that Sam seemed to be on the same "track" as Bundy and with further triggers, may be at the brink of "snapping." I thought we might have a unique opportunity to help him.

Since Sam already demonstrated animosity toward me, it might be possible to create a scenario to notify him of the negative FBI letter in an environment designed to heighten his anxiety. I had already suggested to A/ASAC Ron that we notify Sam of the negative letter in person and have agents available to assist if necessary. It would be easy to further build on that concept.

As A/ASAC Ron had instructed, I met with Sam's professor to let him know that because of my safety concerns about Sam, the negative letter would be placed in Sam's FBI file and the professor could decide if the dean should be notified. I also gave him a copy of the Internet information I printed and told him after finding these similarities, I was even more concerned.

The professor called me the following day and asked if A/ASAC Ron had seen the Internet information I printed. I told him A/ASAC Ron had everything but the Internet information. Because the professor felt it should be seen, I told him I would take it to Blain, the Houston polygrapher. His experience made him the closest thing to an "expert" in the FBI Houston office. Blain was the senior polygraph examiner, had successfully interrogated pedophiles and other criminals and was a certified police instructor having taught on FBI interviewing and interrogation. He was also pursuing his master's degree in psychology and I heard him speak several times about abnormal behavior. If Blain felt this information should be re-addressed with A/ASAC Ron, I would ask him to present it with me.

When I took the loose information to Blain, he had numerous questions and I found it hard to locate the documents he requested. I told him I would organize the information (which I did in notebook sections) and then return it to him for review. I also put in writing that if he had concerns, I recommended that we both meet with A/ASAC Ron before any action was taken. He said he would look at the information over the next few days and give me a call. I also called a friend of mine, a retired expert FBI BAU profiler I had worked with on a major FBI case. He still consulted for the FBI and I asked him (once approved), if he would be willing to give his assessment of a student I had serious concerns about. He was more than willing to assist in any way possible.

Several days later Blain and I discussed the information he reviewed. He understood why I had personal safety concerns and how
Sam could perceive me as his "bad guy" but he did not want to push
him. Blain recommended that he and A/ASAC Ron meet with Sam.
A/ASAC Ron could explain that the decisions were made by the FBI
(not just me) and Sam could ask any questions. Blain would attend the
meeting to observe Sam's behavior. Blain said he would be in Quantico the following week so he asked that I arrange the meeting for the
week he returned.

The next day ADC Keith asked to see me and said CDC Curt was
fuming mad that I asked Blain for his opinion about Sam. ADC Keith
told me to drop it. He said no one would look at anything about Sam
and that was the end of it. I disagreed whole-heartedly but I knew
there was nothing more that could be done.

I called my retired BAU friend and told him that the FBI would not
look into my concerns about the student and I was struggling with the
responsibility of the knowledge I had about him. If this student was
dangerous and others were injured or killed in the future, I needed to
be able to look back and know I did everything possible to stop it
when we had the chance. He assured me that I had done everything I
could, I ran it up every flag pole and shot off the flares – my responsibility in this was over. I knew he was right but I hoped that I would
feel that way in years to come. Would grieving family members feel I
did everything possible?

I found this situation bizarre! So many people became upset every
time Sam's name was mentioned. I was the one treated unfairly and
was the only one that had a reason to be angry. Yet it seemed that I
was also the only one thinking clearly and approaching the situations
with an objective eye. CDC Curt was suggesting that Sam hurt me so
I was out to get him in some way. That thinking was ludicrous. I did
everything possible to get Sam through the FBI program and only denied his extension with concurrence by ADC Keith and Sam's
professor. Sam's disturbances caused a hiccup in my position as IPC –
but I wasn't mad at Sam . . . I was scared of him.

FBI Houston has a document at the Reception Desk and the Duty
Agent Desk called the "Lookout List." Inside the FBI it's referred to
as the "Nut List." Because people walk into the FBI office to make
complaints, a "Duty Agent" is available during working hours to meet
with them. Most encounters are thirty minutes to an hour in length

and trained Special Agents make negative assessments regarding potential danger and mental stability, noting their observations. Derogatory actions were taken against me for expressing my negative opinion of an individual I observed for <u>eleven weeks</u>.

I also find it interesting that the tragedy of September 11, 2001 left the entire country on "alert" for individuals who exhibit similar behavior as the terrorists that caused those catastrophes. Blain told me of one case that was active at the time: 1) a foreign male, 2) was recording a videotape of his wife on a beach, and 3) he panned the camera to a nearby airport and up to a passing plane. This didn't even happen on US soil but the FBI Director, CIA Director and Director of Homeland Security were receiving daily briefings about this case and the man was subjected to two FBI polygraph examinations . . . all because of three similarities to the terrorists.

In the same "alert" status, I recognized an individual with ***47 similarities*** to a historical US killer and no FBI officials would even look at it to make an expert assessment. It just didn't make sense!

I could only come up with two explanations for this: 1) I am not a man. I realize that it was difficult that I recognized things not even on their radar but issues were also identified by Sam's college professor and most of the intern group. This situation was about protecting lives, not about over-inflated male egos, and 2) Sam indeed had powerful "connections." Regardless of the situation, I did not mention Sam's name again.

Five days later, CDC Curt called me into A/ASAC Ron's office and said I was removed as the IPC (again). He said I disobeyed direct orders "not to talk to the university professor" and I was insubordinate. I looked at A/ASAC Ron in disbelief and said, "You told me to meet with the professor." CDC Curt cut me off and said this was not a discussion, the decision was made and the SAC was aware of it. I asked why I was being punished for doing what I was told to do! CDC Curt said I was not being punished. The IPC was a collateral duty that would be reassigned and I would continue my regular full-time duties.

   *   *An interesting note: My EEO case was inactive for an inordinate amount of time and became active <u>just prior</u> to CDC Curt's actions against me.*

I felt like I had been kicked in the gut . . . again. I had no understanding as to why this was happening . . . and no one would discuss it with me. I was hurt and angry that I was being treated so unfairly and even more upset that I had been falsely accused of insubordination by a man that had no involvement in the situation what-so-ever.

After calming down for several weeks, I met with the EEO counselor (who told me he was A/ASAC Ron's basketball buddy). He had a meeting with A/ASAC Ron who said he clearly remembered what he told me and insubordination was never the case. He said CDC Curt was a "hot head" and was just "blowing off steam."

Shortly thereafter (with no IPC named), I met with A/ASAC Ron to give him several outstanding intern matters that needed to be finalized for the previous semester – things that had been scheduled for completion the day I was removed. He asked me to complete the matters we discussed.

He then said that he didn't know if I ever wanted to hear about college kids after what had happened to me, but he asked if I would consider working as the IPC again. He said he wanted to get me back where I belonged. He knew I had poured my heart and soul into the interns and the intern program. I told him that I was very hurt by the way I had been treated (especially by him) but my goal was still to help wherever and however I could.

ҩ҂ҩ҂ҩ҂ҩ

I'm writing this chapter just three weeks after 23 year old college student Seung-Hui Cho killed 32 people and wounded many more at Virginia Tech. His strange (and sometimes dangerous) behavior was identified years before his killing spree. Lucinda Roy, the former chair**woman** of Virginia Tech's English department had serious safety concerns about Cho. She went to police and other university officials to seek help, but nothing was ever done.
(www.cnn.com/2007/US/04/17/vtech.shooting/index.html).

What does it take to get law enforcement to act? If the FBI won't take action on documented incidents from one of their own . . . can the public really expect to get their attention?

It is important to remember . . .

♦ Columbine High School Massacre in April 1999 where twelve classmates and one teacher died at the hands of Eric Harris (age 18) and Dylan Klebold (age 17)

♦ The shooting at Santana High School in March 2001 when Charles Andrew Williams (age 15) killed two and wounding thirteen

♦ John Jason McLaughlin (age 15) who murdered two classmates at Rocori High School in September 2003

♦ Richard Ramirez (age 24 when he committed his first murder) – being found guilty of 13 counts of murder, five attempted murders, 11 sexual assaults and 14 burglaries when he was tried at age 29

♦ Robert Charles Browne, who served in the US Army and admitted to murdering up to 49 people, starting at the age of 17 and continuing for the next 25 years

♦ Ted Bundy, who was very intelligent, was often described as educated, charming and articulate. His first known and confirmed murders were committed when he was 27 and continuing for five years for an estimated total of 30 to 100 (actual numbers not known)

♦ Jeffrey Lionel Dahmer, with service in the US Army, was 18 when he started his gruesome killings of 17 men and boys which lasted 13 years

♦ Edmund Emil Kemper III killed his grandparents at the age of 16 and went on to kill six females, his mother and one of her friends over the next nine years

♦ Coral Eugene Watts, who committed as many as 100 murders between the ages of 22 and 29

I stand by my assessment of Sam and believe he is a walking time bomb. If he stays on his current path, I believe we will see him in the years to come . . . with devastation in his wake.

❧❧❧❧❧❧❧

"There is nothing to fear except the persistent refusal to find out the truth, the persistent refusal to analyze the causes of happenings." ~ Dorothy Thompson

~ *10* ~

Battling FBI Lies

"To stand in silence when they should be protesting
makes cowards out of men." ~ Abraham Lincoln

ᘉᘉᘉᘉᘉᘉᘉ

Eleven (11) months after I requested the Albuquerque Career Board cassette tape, I was notified that the FBI lost it. However, it mysteriously arrived by mail in March 2002. By then, I was beginning to put the nightmare of Albuquerque behind me. I was feeling better physically and I enjoyed working in the Houston division.

I felt humiliated, hurt and disrespected when I listened to that Career Board tape. Knowing they were being recorded, supervisors completely ignored my qualifications and made derogatory personal comments about me, making it clear that they would not permit me to go anywhere in management. Barry and a female supervisor adamantly objected to the comments and discussion taking place but they were not able to stop it seeing that the ASAC himself (the Career Board Chairman) was instigating the grossly inappropriate (and false) statements.

Though I'd tried to put Albuquerque behind me, the tape brought it front and center. Those supervisors violated FBI policy and they violated the law - my personal rights as a female employee.

I struggled with the decision of what to do. They couldn't hurt me any more since I had been transferred to Houston . . . but if I did nothing, they would only continue their antics toward their next victim.

I remembered the female agent that stood up before I got to Albuquerque. She won an EEO settlement against the FBI, was transferred to another FBI office and the judge ordered that posters be displayed throughout the office, "This Office Condones Sexual Harassment." I contacted her and asked about her case.

Though I suffered from gender discrimination as a female agent, she had suffered from sexual harassment with dozens of documented incidents. One agent put a mirror on his shoe so he could look up her dress - - - male agents continuously groped and grabbed her - - - and one male agent pulled her face into his crotch while making lewd comments. I couldn't believe what she endured. She stood up for what was right and helped those that came after her - - - including me. I hadn't experience the same types of behavior. However, the men continued in their harassment – they just changed tactics.

How could I continue to tell people working with the FBI to stand up and do the right thing if I was not willing to do that myself? How would I feel if I knew another woman had to go through the same treatment I endured because I took the easy road and did nothing? I thought of it like a rape . . . if you don't hold violators accountable, it is very likely they will go on to commit the same act. I had numerous reasons to "do the right thing." The only reason I could find not to go forward was that it would be difficult for me. That is exactly why so many people won't do the right thing . . . because their focus stays on themselves . . . not on helping others. As I thought about my life and what I had always been most proud of - - - it was clear - - -

Do the right thing even when it's hard!

Like a muddied spring or a polluted well is a righteous man who gives way to the wicked. Proverbs 25:26 (NIV)

After a lot of prayer I filed an EEO complaint based on the discriminatory actions of the Albuquerque supervisors evidenced on the cassette tape. Unfortunately there is no way I could isolate the case only against FBI Albuquerque - it had to be against the FBI as a whole.

Over one year later (June 2003) I was notified that the FBI dismissed my EEO complaint. They didn't deny that I had suffered discrimination; in fact they argued that I should've known I had been discriminated against before I got the tape. They stated that the FBI's failure to provide the tape for a year wasn't the issue; they claimed that I failed to file my complaint "in a timely manner" and with that it was dismissed. My only recourse was to file the matter civilly against the Department of Justice: Tracy L. Baldwin vs. Attorney General John Ashcroft (later changed to Alberto R. Gonzales).

I must be the most naïve person on the planet when it comes to my government and the FBI. I actually believed what my government told me . . . that I have a legal right to stand up for myself when I have suffered discrimination. They go on to say that I will be protected from retaliation:

> *An employer may not fire, demote, harass or otherwise*
> *"retaliate" against an individual for filing a charge of*
> *discrimination, participating in a discrimination proceeding,*
> *or otherwise opposing discrimination.*
>
> www.eeoc.gov/types/retaliation.html

Just over one month after the FBI dismissed my EEO claim, the FBI tried to end my career. In August 2003, I received information that the Medical Mandates Board at FBI HQ was reviewing my medical file. The FBI's Health Care Program and FBI HQ Office of General Counsel were going to determine if I should: 1) be removed as a Special Agent, 2) apply for medical disability retirement, 3) be reassigned to a support position, or 4) seek Worker's Compensation Benefits. * *Notice that remaining a Special Agent was not an option.*

I went to my supervisor and he, my ASAC and the SAC wrote the following to FBI HQ . . . and saved my career:

> *"While on limited duty, SA Baldwin has been a terrific asset*
> *for the Houston Division. She has constantly shown a good*
> *work attitude and has helped out in many capacities. SA*
> *Baldwin has been performing at one hundred per cent of her*
> *assigned duties.*
>
> *Upon her return to work, SA Baldwin was initially assigned to*
> *work drug-related matters. Based upon a temporary person-*
> *nel reorganization, SA Baldwin was assigned to the division's*
> *Administrative squad in late October, 2002. Her primary re-*
> *sponsibility was to address incoming applicant leads and*
> *SPIN matters in Headquarters City territory. In performing*
> *her mission, it was not uncommon for SA Baldwin to receive a*
> *large volume of leads with short deadlines. By way of exam-*

ple, she recently completed an investigation regarding a US District Court nominee. Initially SA Baldwin was given a three-week deadline to conduct numerous interviews in this matter. Upon completion of the initial investigation, FBI Headquarters requested an additional 28 interviews and background checks to be conducted in less than 48 hours, in order for a nomination to go before Congress prior to an up- coming recess. Although she was on sick leave at the time, SA Baldwin readily reported to duty, completing all interviews assigned and served as a mentor to three probationary agents in meeting the short deadline. Based on her exemplary per- formance, the Special Inquiry and General Background Investigations Unit said this about SA Baldwin, "you did an excellent job in putting this together. I know that it has been a real pain, with deadlines and other assignments."

Another example of SA Baldwin's dedication to duty and pro- fessionalism was an investigation with a five-day deadline involving a candidate for US Circuit Court. SA Baldwin's work was recognized by an Assistant Director who wrote in a letter to the Houston SAC, "the completed investigation was thorough, well written and conveyed all the appropriate issues in an exceptional manner, in spite of the short time con- straints." The work product produced by SA Baldwin did not require changes or corrections by her immediate supervisor and her reports were concise and conveyed facts needed by FBIHQ to make appropriate decisions in sensitive SPIN/applicant investigations. Her work and professionalism were more than indicative of the performance of an experi- enced GS-13 investigative agent preparing documents for use at the highest levels of government.

In addition to conducting applicant investigations, SA Baldwin voluntarily participated in a number of anti-drug presenta- tions to local area schools. Recognizing the need to update the division's anti-drug presentation, SA Baldwin independ- ently coordinated with FBIHQ, DEA, the Houston Police Department, and the Humble Police Department, in creating an up-to-date anti-drug presentation. By taking the initiative in this matter, SA Baldwin once again displayed those traits that are expected regarding the performance level of a GS-13 investigative agent.

Finally, SA Baldwin eagerly assisted the Houston Office during the Columbia Shuttle disaster and recovery, volunteering for shifts at the NASA Command Post. During the days that she was not working at the NASA CP, she volunteered to cover weekend duty shifts for other agents who were assisting with Shuttle recovery efforts.

In summary, during her assignment to the Houston Division Administrative squad, SA Baldwin met or exceeded expectations in all of her given assignments and performed her duties at a skill level commensurate with that of a veteran GS-13 Special Agent. It is recommended that SA Baldwin continue on limited duty as an FBI Agent until she is approved for full duty."

I am extremely grateful that the Houston upper management stepped up to defend me. It was very unfortunate for me that just one year later the supervisor had been reassigned, the ASAC was no longer in the Houston division and the SAC had retired.

My EEO case remained dormant until the summer of 2004 and then became extremely active. I found myself in a full court press. I worked with an exceptional attorney, Charles T. Jeremiah in Houston and traveled to Albuquerque and Washington DC for depositions.

CDC Curt was known to be vindictive and spiteful and he didn't like EEO cases or people speaking against the FBI. Unfortunately, I was responsible to report my attorney contacts to the CDC so he had full knowledge of every step of my EEO case. He was condescending throughout my interactions with him, demonstrating disgust in his tone and manner toward me. When he gave me my personnel file (requested through FOIPA) I asked if it was now "open" information. He replied, "You can go wipe your butt with it." He also had direct and frequent contact with his chain-of-command . . . the <u>FBI HQ Office of General Counsel</u> in Washington DC.

FBI Headquarters (HQ) Upper Level Organizational Structure

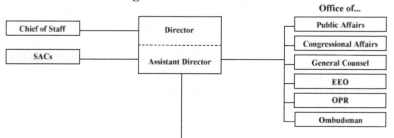

www.fbi.gov/page2/july06/orgchart072606.pdf

Looking back it should not have been a surprise that CDC Curt had been so angry toward me regarding the interns or anything else for that matter. However, I was shocked when I was notified that he filed false allegations with OPR about me:

1) Conducted an unauthorized investigation of an FBI intern; *(in reference to me using my home computer to "Google" information on the World Wide Web – WWW - accessing the public Internet to educate myself about negatively influential people).*

2) Engaged in unprofessional conduct and unauthorized disclosure by releasing information on an FBI intern to the intern's university without authority; *(I was given a direct order by A/ASAC Ron to meet with my approved university counterpart. The only additional "information" was pages printed off the WWW – open and public Internet).*

3) Engaged in insubordination when you failed to comply with a direct order from the Acting/Assistant Special Agent in Charge (A/ASAC Ron) to discontinue any further inquiry or investigation regarding the intern. *(I was never given such an order from A/ASAC Ron and was not physically in the FBI office when CDC Curt alleges I was given this order).*

Later a fireable allegation was added . . .

4) Lied under oath during the course of the Administrative Inquiry *(The FBI's characterization because I adamantly denied the above allegations and gave supporting evidence to prove my case).*

I couldn't believe what I was reading. How in the world could CDC Curt make such atrocious allegations? . . . Especially when he was not even personally involved in the situation! As I said before, anyone can make allegations to OPR and I knew CDC Curt was out to "get me." His lies made me angry, but I also felt confident that once OPR did an investigation and found the truth - - - all of this would be behind me.

The OPR process is "confidential." I was required to sign an FBI document stating that I would not discuss the matter with anyone but the OPR investigators from <u>FBI HQ</u>. That meant I was not permitted to speak to the SAC, A/ASAC Ron or anyone else about how preposterous these allegations were. Did they even know CDC Curt had done this? If so, why had A/ASAC Ron permitted it when he knew the truth? I was being railroaded and was completely alone. Apparently CDC Curt had not kept the matter "confidential" because I started getting questions from other agents, bewildered that I was under an OPR. The FBI's inability to be "confidential" remains a long-standing joke. I held to my responsibility regarding "confidentiality" and did not discuss the matter.

I actually got a chuckle when several of the agents told me that the word circulating around the office was that CDC Curt had put me under OPR for having interns do yard work at my home. Unlike the lies CDC Curt made up – the yard work actually happened – and had nothing to do with the OPR. The interns were always talking about their need for money and what a hardship it was that they didn't receive pay while working at the FBI. When I needed landscaping help in my back yard, I talked to ADC Keith and told him that I have a yard service but needed some extra work done. I thought of asking interns for their assistance and wanted to be sure that would not be a problem with the FBI. ADC Keith said it was really great that I thought of the interns and it would be no problem to ask for their help as long as they knew it was separate and apart from the internship. With ADC Keith's approval, three of the interns helped me one evening after work.

During the discovery process for the EEO case, all of my Albuquerque personnel files were provided and every aspect of my performance was intensely scrutinized. The documentation clearly evidenced that my performance had remained exceptional even in the midst of the unfair treatment I endured.

I traveled to Albuquerque for depositions in February 2005 and imagine my shock when I was asked questions about the Houston OPR by the Albuquerque AUSA defending the FBI against my allegations of mistreatment. Initial interviews had not even been completed about the Houston OPR, much less any investigation conducted.

Then things started to make sense. My EEO complaint was originally dismissed by the FBI HQ EEO (no doubt with assistance from the FBI HQ Office of General Counsel) located in Washington, DC. I exercised my legal right and filed it as a civil matter against the Department of Justice (DOJ). As the Houston CDC, Curt has contact with the FBI HQ Office of General Counsel frequently, as well as FBI HQ OPR. In fact he talks to them about every Houston OPR investigation opened (and there were a lot of them). CDC Curt didn't like that I had an EEO case so he fabricated an OPR against me and filed it with his buddies at FBI HQ. The FBI agent assigned to assist the Albuquerque AUSA was the Assistant General Counsel, Employment Law Unit I, FBI HQ Office of the General Counsel.

So how does an AUSA located where the EEO offenses occurred - Albuquerque, N.M. know about a confidential OPR in the Houston Office filed four years after I left Albuquerque? Yep . . . the FBI HQ Office of General Counsel! The FBI has no oversight and lacks the necessary checks and balances to ensure they don't make up their own rules - blatantly dismissive of law.

The EEO case was difficult and even the DOJ tried to dismiss it. However, the Honorable John Parker denied the DOJ finding fact issues for the jury to decide. I settled the case before trial and the FBI paid me $50,000, gave me 40 hours of vacation time and they offered to destroy the documents surrounding the EEO case. Isn't it interesting that the FBI is more than willing to destroy the trail of their wrongdoing? You can find out more about the EEO process by reading my book, *The EEO Process, Where's My Parade!* available through www.eeoinfo.com.

I was released from limited duty in January 2005 and I received my FBI settlement money and vacation time in July 2005. I felt like I was back on a level playing field. "They" mistreated me, I stood up and brought wrongdoing to light – "they" were found to be wrong – now let's get on about the business of the FBI. After paying legal costs and attorney fees, the settlement money came close to paying off my car wreck debt. I could finally see the light at the end of the tunnel . . .

Ooops – it's a train!

❧❧❧❧❧❧

"Truth is not only violated by falsehood; it may be outraged by silence." ~ *Henri-Frédéric Amiel*

❧❧❧❧❧❧

It had been five months since I received my EEO settlement money from the FBI. I had only been back from a Christmas family vacation for one day when I was called in to the ASACs office, a woman fairly new to the Houston office.

I fully expected it to be about the OPR. Even though I did nothing wrong, I was sure they'd hand down some punishment because the lies came from . . . CDC Curt. I remember praying before I drove over to the main office. I knew that God and I together could handle anything that happened. I also prayed that God would give me strength to handle the situation with grace, poise and professionalism.

The meeting was with the new ASAC and CDC Curt (my accuser). I had only spoken to this ASAC passing in the halls and I remember telling her that it was the first time I'd ever seen her office. CDC Curt said this was about the OPR and it wasn't good news (I find that to be an interesting statement seeing that he was getting exactly what he orchestrated). I was handed a barrage of documents and instantly fell into a time warp. This couldn't be real! They were proposing my dismissal?! The FBI is supposed to get to the truth. How could they be making this decision? I remember saying two things: 1) oh, my God, and 2) is this about the EEO? CDC Curt said, "What EEO?" I looked at him in disbelief. Even in front of the ASAC, he was playing dumb and lying.

I later learned that though <u>FBI HQ OPR</u> has the responsibility to investigate allegations of wrongdoing and decide any punishment . . .

in my case it was CDC Curt that *"proposed my dismissal."* I was un-ceremoniously thrown out the door. That was CDC Curt's objective when he fabricated and penned lies to OPR - and his mission was ac-complished. In the blink of an eye, I went from being gainfully employed with a salary of over $100,000 per year - to being unem-ployed with an income of $0.

I know what you must be thinking . . . did she shoot a good guy? Was she using drugs? What in the world did she do to get dismissed from the FBI? You have already read the entire story but the real an-swer is simple . . . I committed the FBI's unpardonable sin - I used my legal rights and stood up when I was mistreated and the FBI was found in the wrong. Let that be a lesson. If you want to keep your job in the FBI, keep your mouth shut and take it . . . whatever "it" is. Do not stand up! Do not tell the truth! And do not do the right thing.

Mr. Jeremiah and I worked together to prepare my written appeal and traveled to Washington, DC to give an oral presentation to the FBI HQ OPR Panel. The case was presented by Mr. Jeremiah and I an-swered questions. It was extremely unpleasant when sarcastic comments were made toward me for being frightened of Sam. One of the officials took great pleasure in snidely asking if I had a gun and if I knew how to use it. I was more than "prayed up" and was able to re-main calm and professional throughout the proceedings.

As part of the process, I was able to review the documents the FBI relied on to make their decision. I was so shocked I felt like I would throw up. CDC Curt had actually manufactured numerous lies and attested to them as truth. He even had the nerve to instigate what I later learned was "Fire the Agent 101." In 2004, CDC Curt wrote a report calling for me to have a psychological fitness for duty examina-tion as soon as possible. I was never told he had done this and was never asked to undergo any type of evaluation. Mr. Jeremiah and I have asked for the document that responded to his request (which would rebut his ridiculous allegations) and as of November 2007, the FBI has still failed to provide it.

As a Special Agent – one of the FBI's own - for nine years, I ex-pected the FBI to do a full investigation of these absurd allegations before ending my career. After all that's what OPR is for - to find the truth. However, in my case, the FBI did not do any investigation - CDC Curt's allegations and plans for dismissal were simply "rubber stamped."

It makes no sense that my reports would be sought after and relied on to evaluate candidates for some of the highest positions in the United States (even throughout the year and some months following CDC Curt's allegations); I was responsible for training all new agents on interview techniques and remained part of the Investigative & Intelligence component for every Houston Command Post operation - yet CDC Curt placed me under OPR investigation and recommended my dismissal for expressing my "negative" opinion of concern regarding a college intern. It doesn't make sense because it isn't logical – CDC Curt's false allegations to OPR were purely used as the tool to end my career with the FBI because I won an EEO settlement against the FBI.

Only after my dismissal did I learn about CDC Curt's scathing report about me and yet he asked for my evaluation assistance with the Intern Program over a year after his allegations. A/ASAC Ron actually provided me with documentation that was used in my appeal, showing he did not support CDC Curt's false statements and efforts against me. A/ASAC Ron also personally told me that he never thought any of this should or would go to OPR but it was not in his hands. Interesting - when he was the FBI Official (the second most powerful in the Houston FBI Division) at the center of CDC Curt's allegations. The OPR strings were rooted well above A/ASAC Ron - at the <u>FBI HQ Office of General Counsel</u>!

Mr. Jeremiah and I clearly showed that the allegations were nothing more than absurd lies and the FBI's actions against me were completely without merit. Thirteen (13) of the FBI's own OPR cases were cited to prove there was no precedent for my dismissal. We also attached more than twenty (20) character letters from various individuals from within the FBI, other law enforcement agencies, civilians, and professionals in communities across the country vouching for my character, honesty and integrity. They further supported that I have an exceptional reputation and have been held in the highest esteem. I consistently demonstrated the character and professionalism of which the Bureau can be proud.

Lying under oath is a serious allegation and a fireable offense. To *further* exonerate myself I <u>offered</u> to take a polygraph examination (in writing on three occasions) and again during the <u>FBI HQ OPR Panel</u> oral presentation. The FBI would not allow me to be polygraphed . . . they simply made false allegations and dismissed me based on lies.

157

That brings to mind two interesting cases . . .

1) A black male agent I personally knew in Houston was under OPR investigation regarding his conduct while assigned at Guantanamo Bay, Cuba. His candor was called into question and he was proposed for dismissal. He traveled to FBI HQ for his oral presentation to the OPR Panel where <u>they asked him</u> to submit to a polygraph examination. He took the polygraph, passed, the OPR was resolved and he resumed his duties as an SA in the FBI Houston office. He has the advantage of protection from unfair treatment by the Black Agents Don't Get Equality (BADGE) 10-year class action lawsuit settlement. Under the agreement approved by US District Judge Thomas Hogan, the FBI is required to overhaul its promotion, evaluation and discipline procedures to address the concerns of black agents.

www.findarticles.com/p/articles/mi_m1355/is_23_99/ai_75021588

2) A male FBI supervisor I know personally from the Wen Ho Lee espionage investigation was placed under OPR. He testified in court <u>under oath</u> and later admitted that he had falsely testified and was forced to retract three key allegations. That agent was still employed as an <u>FBI supervisor</u> until he retired in September 2007.

An American citizen may be "innocent until proven guilty" - However, as a female FBI Special Agent I was "guilty - my innocence ignored."

> *"Special Agent Tracy L. Baldwin is a very valuable asset to the Federal Bureau of Investigation. She possesses many unique talents and skills, a tireless work ethic, and a devotion to her career and country that cannot reasonably be called into question. She has demonstrated over and over her honesty, integrity, and loyalty to the Bureau and has many outstanding accomplishments. Dismissal of an agent of Baldwin's caliber, capabilities and character would be a loss and detriment to the Bureau and the United States of America."*
> *– Charles T. Jeremiah, Attorney at Law*

~ *A Must See* ~

The Intern Coordinators since my tenure have made some . . . interesting decisions! An intern group was authorized to use FBI time, FBI personnel and FBI resources to produce a ~ 30 minute video that made an absolute mockery of the FBI. To mention only a few incidents depicted in this video:

1) An intern was tied up and gagged to simulate Hannibal Lecter from "The Silence of the Lambs" movie. He was rolled out of the FBI vault (located in the CDC Curt's work area) on a dolly.

2) The Security Officers were filmed fist fighting to see who would get to send the turbulent e-mail stating that an employee no longer had access to the FBI Houston building.

3) A married SWAT member was filmed on a couch making and receiving sexual advances from a female intern.

4) The interns were permitted to mock FBI Director Mueller by using his photograph (normally displayed in the employee entrance hallway) while they filmed a "stakeout" where they were distracted from their professional duties.

This video was distributed openly to the intern group, intern Universities, FBI and other personnel.

❧❧❧❧❧❧

The wrath of God is being revealed from heaven against all the godlessness and wickedness of men who suppress the truth by their wickedness; Romans 1:18 (NIV)

❧ *11* ❧

Women Need Not Apply

*The FBI's courtship of women is very "traditional" . . .
the goal being to entice a commitment, not to sustain a
relationship.*

❧❧❧❧❧❧❧

What we now know as the FBI began in 1908 as the Special Agent Force. In 1923 it was known as the Bureau of Investigation and there were actually two female SAs on board; Jessie Duckstein and Alaska Davidson. How coincidental that J. Edgar Hoover became the Director in 1924 and both females resigned - hmmmmmmmm. Hoover was the FBI Director for the next 48 years and allowed no female SAs. He died on May 2, 1972 and the FBI's website states that female SAs applied in spring 1972 and were appointed in August 1972. What an interesting twist that Hoover had such an aversion to women as SAs when it has been widely reported that he wore women's clothes and was a homosexual (*Official and Confidential: The Secret Life of J. Edgar Hoover* (1993) - Anthony Summers, and . . .
www.crimelibrary.com/gangsters_outlaws/cops_others/hoover/6.html.

He wasn't the "man's man" he portrayed to the public and required of his agent workforce. Perhaps that is where the FBI's duplicity is rooted. Today the FBI projects an image to the public that is in sharp contrast to who they really are on the inside.

Having been on the inside until 2006, I can tell you that it is indeed an unwelcoming, male-dominated organization. Women, don't be duped . . . it hasn't changed from its roots under Hoover's dictatorship. The romance writing on the FBI's website parallels the wooing done by criminals/con artists and pedophiles to attract unsuspecting innocents.   You'll   see   things   like   "women   have   gender-related

160

characteristics and talents that make their contribution to law enforcement invaluable," and "females are more able to detect subtle changes in facial expression, which would make them better able to sense moods in other people" (believe me, if you mention "mood" in the FBI, they'll ask if it's "that time of the month"). There's also the claim that women "are more efficient at moving between different ways of relating to the world" (translated in FBI male-speak, it means in your prior experience, you must've 'gotten around'). Please don't buy into the FBI's courting ritual . . . it is purely a facade.

A book of interest from former female SA Rosemary Dew - *No Backup, My Life as a Female FBI Special Agent* offers insight from 1977 through 1990. I was in the FBI from 1997 through 2006. It hasn't changed. The FBI has a revolving door of female SAs because they beckon women to join and once in, treat them so badly they quit or as in my case (and many others) – fabricate lies for dismissal. It would be very interesting to conduct a study on how many female SAs reach retirement. The FBI, in its arrogance, suggests only that women go out to start their own businesses or leave to start families. There may be some women that leave for those reasons but it's definitely not the case with the former female SAs I know.

Many male SAs still don't think women should be FBI agents, even after women having been in the SA ranks for 35 years. They continue to support Hoover in the crusade to keep women "out." They may not be able to stop women from being hired because of what they deem silly "laws," but they can certainly alienate them once they arrive on man-turf . . . it's very similar to the bullies on the playground. Women as secretaries, receptionists, file clerks or general 'step-n-fetch-its' are fine but they do not have to embrace women in the "equal" position of Special Agent.

I have very traditional values regarding the roles of men and women - in personal relationships. However, the women that become FBI SAs work even harder than their male counterparts to succeed in the male-dominated world of the FBI. In 2006, women made up only 18% of the SA population. With persistence and continued efforts, it is my hope that the American public will require the FBI to cease their ingrown discrimination and female SAs will receive equal treatment.

The following article is located on the FBI's website at www.fbijobs.gov/041.asp. My comments to SA Knights statements are identified with bracketed bold and italic text.

SA Knights article is reprinted verbatim (to include his typing errors).

Why the FBI Seeks More Women as Special Agents?

By Special Agent James J. Knights
FBI Applicant Coordinator Pittsburgh PA

Ed note: Many women on campus have decided to leave academe to start their own business, focus on their families or follow their passions. Here's another alternative.

In seeking educated and accomplished professionals to be Special Agents, the FBI has always had difficulty in attracting qualified women. *[I submit that many women research the viability of the FBI as a positive female career. Armed with accurate (rather than recruiter) information, these intelligent women opt for careers that offer fairness and opportunities for advancement. Also, see comments below about 'qualified women.']*

Of 11,649 current Special Agents, only 2,105 or 18% are women. Among the 15,792 FBI support employees, 10,589, or 67%, are women. Clearly, women are well represented in the "traditionally female" non-agent positions, but are significantly under-represented in the "traditionally male" position of Special Agent. *[With women in the ranks as FBI Special Agents for the past 35 years, it is interesting that SA Knights continues to perpetuate the FBI's culture of what they consider "traditional" roles even here.]*

Despite our best efforts here in Pittsburgh and in the 55 other FBI field offices, relatively few qualified women apply to become Special Agents. *[This statement suggests that there are women applying – but the FBI has determined they are not qualified. To my knowledge, most qualified female applicants are rejected at the*

Phase II Interview. It would be interesting to review that subjective process – and the audiocassette tapes made during each interview and determine the male/female composition of the Interview Assessors. A woman was on my Phase II Interview panel and I passed. How many all male panels pass female candidates? Another interesting note is that while assigned in the Houston Division, I applied and was notified I received the position of Phase II Assessor. However, I was never scheduled for the required training.] Why? Do women view the FBI as an unwelcoming, male-dominated organization? *[Women . . . look closely at the tone of his statement. He is telling you how it is. Though posed as a question, it is much like admitting police officers treat urban African American males as criminals. Though laws oppose racial profiling and the internal agency Public Relations machines crank out warm, fuzzy statements . . . the truth remains that racial and gender profiling is thriving.]* Are women averse to carrying and using firearms, or the possibility of physical violence?

Women themselves have told me, "I'm not qualified"; "you wouldn't want me"; "you wouldn't trust me with secret information"; "I can't shoot a gun"; "I can't do the physical training." In reality, many of these women are qualified to be an FBI Special Agent in the premier law enforcement agency in the world. *[Who has he been talking to and are any of these females over the age of 12? The women I know would never make these statements, regardless of their interest in the FBI.]*

The purpose of this article is to explain why women belong in law enforcement and how their unique skills contribution to the mission of the FBI as Special Agents. Women have gender-related characteristics and talents that make their contribution to law enforcement invaluable. *[This is total BS (Bluff-n-Stuff) . . . recruiter and public relations/media talk.]*

What does it take to be a Special Agent?

In addition to having a four-year degree, applicants must be U.S. citizens between the ages of 23 and 36, in good health and physical condition, and able to pass a polygraph test and background investigation. Details are on the FBI's employment Website, www.fbijobs.com

What academic preparation is the FBI looking for today? Many younger people incorrectly believe they should major in a field related to law enforcement.

After the terrorist attacks of September 11, 2001, the FBI changed its priorities in hiring Special Agents. Today, the FBI seeks agents with degrees in computer science, traditional engineering, traditional physical sciences, accounting, (disciplines requiring a mind trained toward logical analysis and critical thinking) or fluency in a critical foreign language, as well as experience in intelligence and counterterrorism. *[Though the FBI may seek these talents and hire based on them, agents (male and female) were <u>rarely</u> assigned to their area of expertise and most 'logical analysis and critical thinking' was done by support analysts, not Special Agents.]*

With Internet and computer-oriented crime on the rise, two years of "computer science and information technology" is a new recruiting category.

Salaries are competitive. New Special Agents earn the equivalent of about $40,000 annually during their 18 weeks at the FBI Academy, and $54,000 to $58,000 after they report to their first field office. After five years, they earn about $80,000 annually.

Why are women exceptionally well-suited?

Research has shown that females are more able to detect subtle changes in facial expression, which would make them better able to sense moods in other people. This is an immensely useful skill for an investigator interviewing someone trying to mislead or manipulate her. *[Again, total BS! Not the fact that females are better suited to these abilities, they are indeed. However, in my experience and in observing other female agents, females are often summarily dismissed when raising these issues in the real world of the FBI.*

For example, I was the Case Agent for a sensitive foreign country matter at a national laboratory. I had observed the subject on numerous occasions and learned what was important to him, his motivations, attitude, demeanor and personality – his "mood" if you will. I developed a solid plan to conduct an interview leading to an interrogation and ultimately a confession.

Two senior agents were then assigned to assist me – which meant they came in and took over. Through my efforts over numerous months and analysis of thousands of documents, I had developed a good case. Now the management didn't trust the 'chic.' I have never been territorial and as a team player I knew the outcome of the case was what mattered and that was more important than my ego being bruised. I explained my observations of the subject and gave the senior agents all my information. This included room set up, the tone that should be used, questions to ask that I already had answers to and the 'hot' questions and how to lead into them. I also outlined how the time should be used for the best results with this subject's personality.

Long story short . . . the two agents were condescending and laughed at me. They told me they knew what they were doing and didn't need my help to get the information/confession. They did things 'their' way for almost two hours and got absolutely nothing! Besides the agents' embarrassment, the national laboratory officials seemed to be embarrassed for them. Their technique was to bully the subject and try to scare him into talking. As I told them earlier, that would not work with this subjects' personality type.

When the two 'experts' were finished, frustrated and ready to leave, I spoke with them in the hall and asked if I could try my approach since it didn't look like we had anything to lose. Throughout my FBI career, I often found myself apologizing for my expertise and success so I wouldn't hurt the fragile male egos around me. It makes me sick to think back on how many male agents flaunted ar-

rogance in their average performance, yet I had to downplay my out-standing achievements.

The agents reluctantly agreed to my suggestion, I think primarily because they saw an opportunity to delight in my failure. However, I was confident with my research and approach and I asked that they sit in particular locations and let me conduct the interview without interruption. The lab officials also sat in the seats I designated for them.

As explanation, every seat in a room has its own 'power' depending on the angle and position to the door, to the table(s) and to the 'power' (or perceived power) of those individuals around them. It was extremely important that this subject be interviewed with me being his only line of sight . . . not toward an exit or toward those he saw as "official power" - or in the case of the other two agents, the perception of "threatening bullies." In less than an hour, I was able to talk to, question and move the subject to tears and a full confession. I treated him with respect and dignity and he remained cooperative. Even after he was dismissed from his position at the lab, I was able to talk him through that transition and he agreed to take a polygraph so I could be sure he was not withholding any additional information or involvement. I never got a positive word from those two senior agents or from any FBI management.]

Another study suggested that women "are more efficient at moving between different ways of relating to the world." In a profession where events and scenarios can change rapidly over a single day or a single hour, such as during kidnapping and extortion investigations, the ability to rapidly and efficiently adapt to different circumstances and regulate how one relates to others is critical. *[Again, he cites studies that may <u>suggest</u> that to be true but in the FBI, female agents are often pushed aside, disregarded or belittled when critical matters arise.*

Here is another personal example. Although I have witnessed numerous female agents in similar situations, many times being called "stupid *******" or worse by male agents, those accounts are being left for them to tell.

The FBI has jurisdiction on federal land so the Albuquerque office was called in when a man went on a rampage and killed four of his relatives on an Indian reservation. One was shot in a pueblo (adobe residence that looks like a mud igloo with one primary room for living/ sleeping and a smaller room used as the kitchen), one was shot just outside the pueblo, and two were shot in their vehicle about half a mile down the dirt road leading to the pueblo.

Although I was assigned to the White Collar Crime squad, in smaller FBI divisions everyone has to work together on a variety of investigations. As difficult as Albuquerque was as a female SA, it was a great place to learn all the different FBI SA work. I was contacted to respond to the scene at 5:00 a.m. and when I arrived at the Command Center (CC), set up at the Tribal Community meeting facility, personnel from numerous law enforcement agencies were coordinating (and arguing about) the response process . . . FBI, DEA, Customs (now Immigration and Customs Enforcement – ICE), Border Patrol, and BIA (Bureau of Indian Affairs – the Indian Reservation police). The media was also on scene with trucks and remote vehicles set up. The area looked like a chaotic bee hive, complete with helicopters buzzing overhead. The FBI SWAT team had already been deployed in search of the shooting subject, still at large.

Though not trained, nor familiar with ERT functions, I was tasked to assist them in recovery of the victims and to process the crime scenes at and near the pueblo. Several hours passed before the area was cleared (of danger) and authorization was given to move from the CC to the crime scenes. During that time, agents conducted interviews and waited for further instructions. Understandably, this tragedy left family members, friends and the Indian community neighbors visibly shaken and upset.

After all the interviews were complete, I went behind the CC to talk with the group of agents that had congregated. I was appalled at how insensitive and crass these men were. They were actually talking about the victims in a flippant manner commenting . . . it's great that they kill each other, then we don't have to - the families are better off with one less drunk mouth to feed – and, it'll save the taxpayers money. I reminded them that the victim family members were close by and the media microphones were extremely sensitive, most likely picking up every word of their conversation. My comment dispersed the 'roaches.'

Later, while still waiting for instruction, I heard ERT members discussing the protective suits needed to process the scene. They were concerned that the bodies, exposed to the sun and extreme heat, would be decaying and cause health risks to ERT personnel. No protective suits had been brought to the scene (so much for our professional, prepared FBI ERT). These discussions continued for about 20 minutes with no resolution. I finally asked where the suits were located (at the office) and volunteered to get them. I immediately left the scene and drove like a maniac, lights and siren (reminiscent of FBI training) to the FBI office to retrieve the protective suits, additional ERT equipment and photographs of the subject.

When I arrived back at the CC, I found that the ERT members had already gone to the crime scene, apparently disregarding the health risks associated with decaying bodies. Because the subject was still at large, only armed agents with body armor were permitted in the area. Many SWAT members were milling around and joking in the CC and the timing worked out for me to ride with them to the crime scene when they were instructed to surround the pueblo perimeter and provide security to the ERT members. I am still shocked at the extreme agent attitudes I observed during this crisis . . . from frantic to lackadaisical. There were very few of us that maintained heightened safety awareness with a professional, calm demeanor.

I delivered the protective suits, which no one used because they said it was "too hot" and I assisted with the victim just outside the pueblo. I worked with a senior agent in placing the victim in a body bag and transporting her to an ambulance. Because rigor mortis had set in, her body was rigid and her fingers scraped against my arm with each step. Though her hand was inside the bag, I still have an uneasy feeling when I think back on it. An interesting note about rigor mortis is that it takes from three to twelve hours for full rigor (specific time dependent on numerous factors) with eventual relaxation at ~ 36 hours.

After placing the body in the ambulance, we got a call to "take cover." An individual was spotted standing on a ridge top with a rifle. Two ambulance personnel were with me, a male and a female, and both were obviously shaken by the call. The male was standing dumbfounded, so I physically forced him to the ground behind the ambulance engine block for protection. The SWAT team apprehended the ridged individual and identified him as a curious bystander . . . yes, a bystander with a rifle!

My next duty was to assist in casting ground impressions, and then to help remove the victim inside the residence, a grandmother who had been shot through the eye. As we all waited to go inside, my head was swimming with questions. I had a tight stomach from the gross comments the male agents were making and I didn't know what to expect when the body was "turned." The agents were saying that the gasses that come out of the body are horrendous, the bodies sometimes 'talk' to you (gurgling sounds) and one extremely foul-mouthed agent said he'd even seen bodies explode. I didn't know what to think. Were the agents just being gross and kidding – or did I need to prepare myself for these things? I knew I wouldn't get serious answers from the guys that were now trying to top each other with gross stories, so I was able to privately speak to the senior agent on scene and let him know that I had never worked with dead bodies before and I was concerned about what kind of reaction I might have. Rather than give me any guidance or assistance, he looked at me with a very stern brow and in a deep voice said, "I'll tell you one thing - - - if you don't do it, I'll fire you right here . . ." (I was listening intently). He continued after a long pause, "Don't throw up on the evidence." With that, he gave out a loud belly laugh and walked off. It felt like time stood still as I sobered to the reality that I would get no help . . . I just had to tough it out (it was only one of thousands of sobering moments). I held my own with every stage of the body recovery . . . and I didn't throw up (which can't be said of all the male agents).

After we finished, I saw agents outside the pueblo locating shell casings and taking measurements. Each point was fully covered by two agents and we got word that the subject had been arrested about a quarter mile from our location . . . returning back to his crime scene. I was later told that he cried out for his mother when he was arrested. One of the male agents told him, "There's no one left to talk to, you killed everyone in your ******* family." He shot them so they wouldn't turn him in on drug charges.

Because we had been working for many hours in the desert heat and I had a break in assignments, I located water and took it to each of the ~ ten team members. I then accompanied US Customs helicopter pilots in picking up agents from a distant drop off point. We all returned to the CC and were released.

It had been a very hard day but I felt a sense of pride and accomplishment for doing my job well. Even in the most difficult of

169

situations, I remained respectful and compassionate for the victims and their families, and I continued to find ways to help my fellow team members.

I'm sure you can imagine my shock and disappointment when, for the next several weeks, male SAs teased and laughed at me as the "water girl."]

Women approach intellectual problems differently than do men. Consider a complex criminal investigation. It has long been accepted that women's verbal skills, including verbal memory and fluency, are superior to men's. In verbal tests, women are better at rapidly identifying matching items. In another area, women were found to rely heavily on the use of landmarks during navigation exercises. Similarly, women are also better able to remember whether items in a sequence had changed places.

These traits indicate that women have the edge in discerning patterns, obviously a critical skill in complex investigations and especially true in using an investigative tool known as "linkage." For instance, while investigating a number of homicides, investigators will often attempt to establish commonalties or "links" between the victims: occupation, age, physical characteristics, residences, friends and associates, even the color of the victims' cars might be considered.

Using linkage in this manner could help determine what drew the killer to those particular victims, which in turn, may help identify him. The advantages of having one or more female investigators at the center of such an investigation are clear. *[Refer to Chapter 9, Facing the Lifeless Eyes of Rage. I discerned patterns and identified 'linkage' about an individual that I (and others) had serious concerns about. Because this was primarily identified by women, FBI management took absolutely no action.]*

Research shows women's cognitive abilities differ in many ways from men's. For the FBI, an investigative team composed of a blend of female and male agents will be much more effective at bringing a complex investigation to a successful resolution quickly and efficiently than would one composed of only one sex. *[Again, more BS! Women's comments are more often summarily dismissed unless they are presented as coming from a male.]*

As a woman, however, your value as an FBI Special Agent goes far beyond differences in brain chemistry. Women's interpersonal skills make them extremely effective law enforcement officers. Women are excellent communicators and listeners, often better able to engender trust among both women and men and defuse and deescalate potentially violent situations, thus avoiding the use of excessive or deadly force. For law enforcement agencies, this might translate into fewer lawsuits. *[It is disconcerting that I demonstrated these abilities (and successes) over and over again, yet each time was a battle to be heard, whereas the male agents (with little or no success) continued to exercise Rambo FBI techniques and be praised by their fellow male agents.]*

Plus, the ability to calm emotionally charged situations may result from female law enforcement officers generally appearing less threatening than men—a definite benefit. In these situations, being a woman is a real advantage. In other words, women possess unique skills that compensate for their being less physically powerful than the men they face in confrontations. *[This comment really struck me. In my experience, female SAs were never permitted to calm situations because the male agents on hand immediately engaged in Rambo mode and intentionally escalated situations. It was a way for them to be 'tough' and feel strong and powerful. Throughout the five years that I participated in arrest operations, I never saw one, not one, done with safety in mind according to FBI procedure. It is sheer dumb luck that agents were not killed. The last sentence should be modified for accuracy . . . In the FBI, women are less powerful than the men.]*

More than one potential female applicant has told me, "I can't kick down doors." My response is: "We don't need you to kick down doors." The FBI has enough agents who are qualified "door kickers." What we need is more agents who have the skills to talk a subject out of a barricaded room, thus eliminating the need to kick down the door in first place and risk lives. *[More BS! I never saw (nor heard of) even one situation where male agents listened to any female agent regarding 'talking to a subject' during an arrest operation. In my experience, male agents dismiss 'talk' as a waste of time.]*

At no time is the ability to communicate, engender trust and have a calming effect more critical than when an FBI Agent is negotiating to save the lives of helpless hostages. The contribution of female agents to non-violent crisis resolution is reflected by the fact that while only 18% of the FBI's nearly 11,700 agents are female, women are 25% of the FBI's 400 hostage negotiators. *[What he doesn't tell you here is that the FBI rarely participates in hostage negotiations. I say rarely because there must be a case (somewhere) when they've done something. While in the Houston division (the fourth largest in the nation), I had a great interest in being a Hostage Negotiator. In doing my 'homework' and reading the Negotiator files (since the team was started) there was not one - none - nada times that the FBI Negotiators did anything!*

Oh, they were deployed with the SWAT team whenever there was a crisis, but they took a back seat to the local police negotiators on each and every occasion. If you are like me, I had to ask why? I knew the team regularly went to various locations for training so I spoke with a senior member of the team and learned that the FBI will not tolerate bad press. The only way to ensure that every opera-

tion is a success for the FBI is not to get involved. They defer to the local police so if there is any heat – the FBI doesn't get burned. The reports are worded to reflect that the team was deployed and on site with an effective resolution. That's called a boondoggle – by definition: a project funded by the federal government out of political favoritism that is of no real value to the community or the nation; to deceive or attempt to deceive; to do work of little or no practical value merely to keep or look busy.

The SWAT teams are very adept at that as well. On numerous occasions, the FBI SWAT team would take their sweet time to arrive at the scene of a crisis. I asked SWAT team members why they were so late in arriving, always after the local police SWAT teams were in position. Again, I was told the FBI will not tolerate bad press. Since these situations often end up being televised, the public will see the FBI present without any embarrassments. I was also told by SWAT members that local police SWAT use rubber bullets (or similar weapons . . . intended to injure but not kill). The FBI can only shoot to stop the threat so every situation where FBI weapons were used would result in death of the subject. Well, apparently the FBI just takes a pass when it comes to crisis resolution. It's also very interesting that the Hostage Negotiator team leader in the Houston office is the only agent (unfortunately a female) that was found to be "Ineffective and Inefficient" during a division Inspection. As far as I know, she's still running the boondoggle team.]

Women are more effective team builders than men. When groups of newly introduced men engage in conversation, they establish a pecking order, perhaps unconsciously. But women converse to cultivate group cohesion.

FBI Special Agents often find themselves working on major cases with other agents they didn't know the day before. Right now, in our medium-sized Pittsburgh Field Office, we're handling two major cases simultaneously—an unprecedented situation. Special Agents and support employees from across the country, who have been sent in to assist in Pittsburgh, suddenly find themselves working alongside strangers. Here's where team-building skills are especially needed. *[At last, he speaks truth. However, the success of big cases regarding the 'team' building is due to agents coming from numerous offices, most often for a 30 to 90 day period. Also, because the normal day-to-day routines and cliques are disrupted by that four letter word - WORK. You'll hear me say a number of times . . . it would truly be amazing what the FBI could accomplish if a professional workplace was enforced and all agents had a good work ethic. I worked two major cases, Eric Rudolf (commonly referred to as the 'bomber') and Wen Ho Lee (commonly referred to as the 'spy'). These experiences were among the best for me in the FBI. No division wants bad reports about the agents they send on travel assignments so many times they will send their best. I was proud to be part of teams that pulled together for a common goal and worked hard. Mind you, those great experiences were the exception, not the rule in FBI cases.]*

What does the FBI offer?

Women in our society—including those who happen to be FBI agents—are still the primary care givers for children. Often they must decide whether to remain on the job or resign to raise a family.

The FBI is attempting to address this problem. The Bureau has always been very supportive of employees in crisis; an agent injured on or off duty—or an employee with a child or spouse suffering from a serious illness— could always count on his or her coworkers and FBI management to go to almost any length give almost any length to assist and support that employee. *[The FBI is notorious for calling itself a 'family.' It is a dysfunctional, abusive family. I have a great family. I joined the FBI as a professional law enforcement agency.*

The above statements are very true regarding male agents. I believe in helping each other, in doing the right thing, easing hardship whenever possible and I have participated in every effort to assist employees. However, the above statements are not only misleading, but actually laughable when it comes to <u>female</u> agents. Below are just a few examples:

- *A male agent and his wife had a baby and an All Employee e-mail was sent to solicit meals to be delivered to his home. He also had the assistance of his mother-in-law, who had moved in with them.*

- *A male agent's wife underwent brain surgery and an All Employee e-mail was sent to solicit meals to be delivered to his home. He was also given a light duty assignment in addition to vast amounts of administrative time (so he would not have to use vacation or sick leave) to care for his wife. His family members were located in the area.*

- *A female agent's husband, an FBI supervisor, was stricken ill and died within a six month period. Nothing employee wide was done for her and her family members were located across the country. She contacted Director Freeh about her situation and he arranged for her to receive a hardship transfer to be closer to her parents (her father being a retired FBI SA). So far so good . . . isn't that a great FBI . . . until she arrived in the new division and was mistreated. After 23 years (as both support and as an outstanding Special Agent), even after presenting cases before Congress, the FBI fabricated lies about her and dismissed her.*

- *A female agent was unable to work for several months due to mononucleosis. Nothing employee wide was done for her.*

- *I was unable to be at work for several weeks due to mononucleosis. Nothing employee wide was done for me and my family lived out of state.*

- *I also underwent two surgeries for kidney stones and because I paid dues as a member of the FBI Recreation Association at the time, I received an arrangement of flowers. Throughout that hardship, I received no assistance from my FBI 'family' and I was not given any 'administrative' considerations. Bear in mind that I did not expect any 'special' treatment but I should be afforded the same considerations as male agents.*

♦ *A male SWAT (added perk) member was diagnosed with cancer. Not only was an All-employee call put out to assist him and his family . . . the SWAT team created a 'bald-eagle' club drive. FBI time was used to gather employees together and bid for people to shave their heads. It was easy to spot the SWAT guys after that - all bald. It was very touching that they did that for him. Employees were also given 'administrative time' to help him through treatments or anything else his family needed.*

♦ *A female agent had also been diagnosed with cancer in the same FBI division. Nothing employee-wide was done for her.*

♦ *I was in a horrific car wreck that you read about in Chapter 7 . . . in my personal car because the SAC told me to use it to save the FBI gas money. Nothing employee-wide was done for me. I was later told that numerous employees suggested at least sending flowers. They were told the FBI could not do that. The employees sent me flowers and cards independently. I couldn't have made it through that time without the care and assistance from my network of incredible friends. I never even received a phone call from the upper management to check on my recovery. My FBI "family" did nothing but make my situation more difficult.*

The rules just aren't the same for males and females – even in times of hardship.]

For example, the FBI has always had a policy of "hardship transfers." An agent with a compelling reason, such as a sick elderly parent with no one else to depend upon, could request a transfer to another field office to be close to that parent. About 10 years ago, the FBI and other federal agencies started a "family friendly" sick leave policy, which allows an employee to use her or his sick leave to care for an ill family member.

The FBI follows the federal Family and Medical Leave Act, which permits employees to take up to 12 weeks of leave without pay for medical exigencies, including the birth and care of a child, placement of a child for adoption or foster care, a serious personal health problem, or the care of a seriously ill parent, spouse or child. The FBI's "voluntary leave transfer program" encourages employees to donate their unused annual leave to their colleagues who, because of serious illness or accident, have used all their available annual and sick leave. Women can use the program to remain out of work to care for a seriously ill family member. In fact, more than half the employees using this program are women. *[My supervisor was bound and determined to make me go without pay, even when several employees offered to donate time for me. One employee filled out the appropriate paperwork and because of my difficult supervisor, the time was not applied until FBI HQ got involved. In fact, after learning of the difficulties I was having with the local office, I was told to speak directly to FBI HQ personnel. Later, two other employees offered to donate time for me and I was told I didn't 'qualify' for the program.*

SA Knights makes a point to highlight that more than half the employees using this program are women. What he doesn't tell you is that the FBI does not grant maternity leave. All the female employees that had babies were put in the position to need time donations so they continued to receive a paycheck.]

Perhaps of greatest benefit to female Special Agents in particular is a policy the FBI started in 1990. In a truly revolutionary move for the bureau, Special Agents were, with justification, given the option of working part-time.

This program allows an agent, say a woman with a pre-school child, to work 16-32 hours a week, thus having the flexibility to raise her child and pursue a career. Of the 219 agents who have opted to work part-time since the program started, 209 are women who were not forced to make the painful choice between career and family. *[The BS here is maddening! The key word in SA Knights prose is "justification" which in the FBI means . . . anything the local management might be feeling at the time. If they like you, they might say yes, if they're having a bad day, they'll say no. I personally know of numerous female agents that had a baby and applied for the part-time program. They were denied based on 'the needs of the Bureau' (a catch phrase excessively used when management doesn't want to approve something but has no basis for their decision). These dynamic, intelligent, trained female Special Agents resigned amid a flurry of frustration and anger. I heard male agents commenting that "Another one bites the dust."*

Something else not mentioned here is that the women, who by some miracle have gotten the nod for part-time hours, are treated like second class citizens. The supervisors and squad mates make no bones about their distaste that the female is 'not carrying her weight' and 'coming and going as they please." As long as the internal culture remains as is, the part-time program will be ineffective and punish those that are permitted to use it.]

Female agents are still trying to balance family and work, and the FBI is doing what it can to help, recognizing the value of a woman in society and that her family responsibilities don't evaporate when she becomes a Special Agent. If it is to attract and retain highly qualified women as Special Agents, the FBI must afford them the flexibility to be law enforcement officers and to fulfill their family responsibilities. *[However, since the FBI is more interested in maintaining the revolving door of female agents, things are working just fine.]*

The best job in the world.

Why be a Special Agent? No other law enforcement agency has the FBI's resources, reputation, prestige and global presence. Consider returning a kidnapped child to her mother, helping put a drug ring out of business, exposing a spy, assisting in the search of a crime scene that is national news, uncovering that critical clue that allows the prevention of the next terrorist attack on us.

Women possess different analytical skills, approach problems differently, and have different talents and abilities than do men. Rather than considering them divisive, the FBI believes these differences are complementary. As a woman, you have valuable contributions to make to your country's security by becoming part of the world's premiere law enforcement agency. The FBI would be even stronger and more effective if more women contributed their unique talents as Special Agents.

If you believe the FBI is a male-dominated organization, you're correct—although less so now than 20 years ago. It will remain so until more qualified women choose to make a difference. The FBI recognizes and acknowledges your value to law enforcement and society. If you believe the FBI should continue to change, here is your opportunity to be the catalyst of that change. The offer is on the table. *[I hope you are starting to recognize the BS on your own now.]*

Thanks to Lorelei Stein, PhD, Point Park University, Pittsburgh, for providing invaluable guidance in research for this article, as well as Joe Zabka, of the Helen Jean Moore Library of Point Park University. Contact Special Agent James Knights at (412) 432-4374 or jknights@leo.gov

*** Note that this article is written by a man with apparently no
female agent input as to its content. With all the female agents
available to give a first hand account of how the FBI operates and
how valuable women are to the FBI – why then, did a female agent
not write this article and post it in a prominent position on the FBI's
website?*

Not all female FBI Special Agents have a difficult time. There are
the lucky *few* who find a champion early on that paves the way for
them. I also recognized four categories of female SAs (identified by
male agents) that seemed to receive "fair" treatment:

1) Women perceived by male SAs as unattractive and/or mascu-
   line.

2) Women living an alternate lifestyle with other women. These
   agents were not seen as any sort of threat by male agents and
   were referred to as "she-males."

3) Women married to male agents, whether those males were employed by the FBI, DEA or Secret Service. Particular
   exception was given to female agents married to agency supervisors.

4) Black women, most probably because they are protected by the
   BADGE (Black Agents Don't Get Equality) 10-year class action lawsuit.

Had I been told all this before I applied to the FBI, I can't say for
sure that I would've believed it could be true in my case. I have
always been extremely successful and worked well with all types of
people, cultures, etc.

With this information in mind, please do your homework before
applying to be an FBI SA. Look up all the EEO lawsuits/cases
initiated due to discrimination and retaliation. Review the information
at www.fbiwhistlestop.com about FBI Whistleblowers and the class
action lawsuits filed (and won) by Hispanic and then Black agents.
Research information about former female SAs such as Jane Turner,
Rosemary Dew, Coleen Rowley and a non-agent by the name of Sibel
Edmonds. Even male agents such as Bassem Youssef, Frederic

Whitehurst, John Roberts, Robert Wright Jr. and Bernardo Perez have paid the price for bringing FBI wrongdoing to light.

Also, read all you can about the FBI to include: *No Backup, My Life as a Female FBI Special Agent* – Rosemary Dew and Pat Pape; *Special Agent: My Life On the Front Lines As a Woman in the FBI* - Candice DeLong; *The FBI: Inside the World's Most Powerful Law Enforcement Agency* - Ronald Kessler; *Hoover's FBI* - William W. Turner; *Unlimited Access* - Gary Aldrich; *FBI Secrets: An Agent's Expose* - M. Wesley Swearingen and anything else you can get your hands on. Once you have the full story, you can make an intelligent decision about applying to the FBI and know what you're getting into.

My only other word of advice comes from an old Kenny Rogers song, The Gambler: *You got to know when to hold 'em, know when to fold 'em, know when to walk away and know when to run.*

The difficulty is in knowing that you are the only person that can see all the cards you've been dealt and you are the only person that can make the right decision for your life. Well, the only person on earth, that is. God can help you make the right decisions and know when you should rest, stop, go, persist, fight for what is right . . . and know when to keep fighting - hard!

I wish you all the best and may God bless you.

ೞೞೞೞೞೞ

"Never continue in a job you don't enjoy. If you're happy in what you're doing, you'll like yourself, you'll have inner peace. And if you have that, along with physical health, you will have had more success than you could possibly have imagined." ~ Johnny Carson

~ *12* ~

The Hand of God in My Darkest Hours

*When you pass through the waters, I will be with you;
and when you pass through the rivers, they will not
sweep over you. When you walk through the fire, you
will not be burned; the flames will not set you ablaze.
Isaiah 43:2(NIV)*

~~~~~~~

I thanked God that I was escorted out of the FBI on a Wednesday
so I could go to the Lakewood Church service that night. In the afternoon, I crossed my garage to get a CD and I slipped on a slick spot and
fell . . . hard. I landed on my knee and my jaw hit the bookcase knob.
I was lucky I didn't put an eye out with all the garden tools! Blood
was running down my leg and I had a knot under my chin.

For a fleeting moment, I thought about just staying home and curl-
ing up in a ball - it had been a very hard day to say the least! But I
resolved that Satan can beat me black and blue - but I was going to
worship the Lord and I was going to church! I remember as I walked
toward the doors to the Church, I said, "The Lord gives and the Lord
takes away - blessed be the Name of the Lord!" *(Job 1:21)*

Lisa Comes (Joel's sister) was speaking on God being with you in
your darkest hour. She articulated how I felt on that very day. My
entire career, what I devoted my life to; where I had literally put my
life on the line serving my country; where I gave blood, sweat and
tears; everything . . . was being jeopardized because of lies.

I didn't have a husband to rely on or help me through this and I felt
very alone. Lisa talked about her darkest hour – when she was told
(after fertility treatments and two surgeries) that she couldn't have
children. She went home and in her bathroom . . . completely broke

down and submitted herself to the Lord. Three months later the call came to adopt her twin girls and then shortly after that, they adopted their little boy. I've never seen her family up on the platform but she brought them up that night.

As I watched her husband and children stand by her side . . . she said, "Look what came out of my darkest hour." That's when I cried for the first time that day! I knew God had me in the palm of His hand and He would be with me in my darkest hours. There would be many of them to come!

For the next three days, my mind was filled with questions about what I should do. I just couldn't wrap my mind around how all this could happen. I didn't do anything wrong and my mind was bombarded with unanswered questions . . . Why was this happening to me? . . . How could this be happening? . . . It's the FBI - they know this isn't true! Why didn't someone step forward and tell the truth?

I thought about putting my house up for sale, selling everything and moving to Alabama to be closer to my parents. My mind was spinning and then I remembered *Psalm 46:10 – "Be still, and know that I am God; I will be exalted among the nations, I will be exalted in the earth."* A very dear Christian man once told me the translation to that verse . . . sit down, shut up and listen.

My life is normally filled with "noise." I don't sleep well when it's quiet so I always have a fan on. When I get up I turn on the radio or TV, I drive with the radio on – even when I'm working, I have a radio or TV on in the background. I realized that God would have to practically scream to get my attention and He often speaks in a still, small voice.

> *And He said, Go out and stand on the mount before the Lord. And behold, the Lord passed by, and a great and strong wind rent the mountains and broke in pieces the rocks before the Lord, but the Lord was not in the wind; and after the wind an earthquake, but the Lord was not in the earthquake; And after the earthquake a fire, but the Lord was not in the fire; and after the fire [a sound of gentle stillness and] a still, small voice.*
> *1 Kings 19: 11-12(AMP)*

Driving down the highway, I turned off the radio and in that silence, God gave me peace and assurance that **I'm not going anywhere . . . I'm exactly where He wants me.** My job was to trust

Him, get closer to Him and let Him resolve this situation by bringing out the truth.

As a Single Adult Bible Study Teacher at Lakewood, I found that my lessons were often in areas that God was teaching me - I was living His Word. For instance, when I taught about the spiritual law of sowing and reaping, I looked over my life and saw that my seeds have been good and pure. I've sown truth, honesty, love, compassion, money, etc. God will not be mocked and I trusted that He would restore me and bring me through this with a double portion of His blessing!

> *Instead of their shame my people will receive a double portion, and instead of disgrace they will rejoice in their inheritance, and so they will inherit a double portion in their land, and everlasting joy will be theirs. Isaiah 61:7(NIV)*

Even falling in my garage, the very first day all this happened, I could see that Satan may make me stumble (blood down my leg) but to keep my chin up (the only way to see the bruise from the bookcase knob) and God will give me strength to get through this.

God knew what I needed even when I didn't and He knew how to deliver it. During Lakewood drama rehearsal I was asked to do a sketch where the script called for me to scream - then get a hug and be told, "I love you." I'm not someone to raise my voice, much less scream, and I didn't realize how much I needed to let it out. When we were finished, I was amazed at how much better I felt! I'm not telling you to scream at people if you're going through a difficult time . . . I'm just saying that God had perfect timing in giving me a safe avenue to vent. As a suggestion, throwing ice at a fence is a great way to get rid of stress - - - no damage, no cleanup.

I had the amazing opportunity to pray with Dodie Osteen, Joel's mother. If you don't know, God miraculously healed Dodie of cancer over 25 years ago. She has a passion and heart for people and she makes herself available to pray with those that are hurting.

Dodie's prayer was powerful – that God's truth and justice would be revealed. Looking back I see that it still hadn't sunk in for me. I didn't understand why God would allow lies to be told and why I had to go through all this . . . but praying with Dodie, I had a peace knowing that God was in control and He would take care of it. This journey may be extremely difficult, but it could be used to encourage others.

> *And we know that God causes all things to work together for good to those who love God, to those who are called according to His purpose.* Romans 8:28 (NIV)

It doesn't say all things but the FBI lies – it says <u>all things</u>. God is truth. It is not in His nature nor is He capable of lying – so I knew in my heart that His word was true. However, in my mind I didn't see how this could be good in any way. The FBI attacked my integrity and character; my reputation - - - the very things I cherish and hold most dear.

Dodie introduced me to John, a former police officer that was now in charge of Lakewood Security. He offered to arrange a time for me to pray with Joel. Because of Lakewood's size, I don't have the opportunity to pray with my pastor like I've had in other churches. It never occurred to me to even ask to pray with Joel but I was grateful that John gave me that opportunity. On January 11, 2006, just one week after I was escorted out of the FBI, Joel prayed with me. His prayer was powerful and he asked God to turn the tide of this battle and resolve the situation with the documents I was preparing. He prayed with confidence that the truth would be revealed and I would be restored. I sat with Dodie and Lisa during that service, behind Victoria (Joel's wife). The Osteen's are anointed and as I sat there with Lakewood's "first family," I felt God's love and strength.

> *But no weapon that is formed against you shall prosper, and every tongue that shall rise against you in judgment you shall show to be in the wrong. This [peace, righteousness, security, triumph over opposition] is the heritage of the servants of the Lord [those in whom the ideal Servant of the Lord is reproduced]; this is the righteousness or the vindication which they obtain from Me [this is that which I impart to them as their justification], says the Lord. Isaiah 54:17 (AMP)*

As the days went on, I wanted to hide and not tell anyone about my situation! I was embarrassed, humiliated and hurt – all because of <u>LIES</u>! Then I realized that this was straight from the pit of hell. CDC Curt wasn't the enemy; he was just a very lost man full of evil being used by Satan, the father of all lies - the great accuser. Satan was attacking what I hold most dear - - - truth! I knew that in God's time, in His way, He would bring me through this and resolve the situation.

You belong to your father, the devil, and you want to carry out your father's desire. He was a murderer from the beginning, not holding to the truth, for there is no truth in him. When he lies, he speaks his native language, for he is a liar and the father of lies. John 8:44 (NIV)

The thief comes only to steal and kill and destroy; I have come that they may have life, and have it to the full. John 10:10 (NIV)

Satan works in darkness, deception and isolation. I recognized that the feelings I had, especially those to withdraw into my house until all this was over, were not from God. God calls His people to be light. Regardless of the allegations brought about by the almighty FBI, I (and they) know the truth and there is absolutely no basis for any shame or embarrassment on my part. They, especially CDC Curt, must answer to God about being a false witness and telling lies.

Do not gloat over me, my enemy! Though I have fallen, I will rise. Though I sit it darkness, the LORD will be my light. Micah 7:8 (NIV)

When Jesus spoke again to the people, he said, "I am the light of the world. Whoever follows Me will never walk in darkness, but will have the light of life." John 8:12 (NIV)

I have come into the world as a light, so that no one who believes in Me should stay in darkness. John 12:46 (NIV)

Therefore judge nothing before the appointed time; wait till the Lord comes. He will bring to light what is hidden in darkness and will expose the motives of men's hearts. At that time each will receive his praise from God. 1 Corinthians 4:5 (NIV)

This was an ongoing battle in my mind. There was no part of this situation that was okay and I felt completely mowed down, stomped on and discarded. I also knew that God had allowed this to happen and I didn't understand why He would do this to me.

Hadn't I been through enough with the Albuquerque situation? . . . Almost being killed in a car wreck and the years of recovery? . . . The difficulties that came with standing up and doing the right thing? . . . Living away from my family and not being married? I had many days and nights of crying out to God in anger for Him allowing all this to happen. He's God! He could fix this and have the truth revealed in a moment. Why hadn't He prevented all these lies? Why wasn't He helping me? Why was he letting me suffer? If He really loved me, He wouldn't let this happen to me! After all the questions and no answers, I stopped fighting and focused on what I could do to resolve the situation. I had to get busy working with Mr. Jeremiah to write my response to the FBI's allegations, collect evidence and resolve this so I could get back to work.

I've always been one to say that God helps those that help themselves . . . but there's more to it than that. Sometimes God helps those that can't help themselves – and sometimes God requires that we take action - keep taking steps forward and continue to stand.

> *Therefore put on the full armor of God, so that when the day of evil comes, you may be able to stand your ground, and after you have done everything, to stand. Ephesians 6:13 (NIV)*

One of the best (and most difficult) things I did was to call people, tell them what happened and ask if they would write a Character Letter for me to include with my written response to the FBI's allegations.

Every person I talked to was outraged at what the FBI did and wanted to help in any way they could. They all wrote amazing letters of support and I found so much comfort in reading those letters in the difficult days to come. They were a source of comfort in times that I felt too weak to reach out. It meant the world to me that these people not only stood by me and supported me, they put it in writing. Over twenty (20) letters were provided to the FBI.

I wish I could tell you that I handled this situation well and completely rested in God's arms but as much as I love the Lord and wanted to lean on Him . . . I was angry to the core of my being and resisted letting that go.

From the day I was escorted out, I was too upset to eat and slept very little. I had a knot in my stomach constantly and every time I thought of food, or got near food, I felt sick and immediately lost 22 pounds. Though I got to my goal weight, starvation is the wrong way to go about it. I lost nearly half of my hair in the months that followed with clumps falling out every time I brushed my hair or showered. My monthly cycle was also affected and I bled for two solid months.

The more stress I felt, the more cigarettes I smoked. During the first three and a half months of this ordeal, I smoked up to three packs a day. Even for a smoker, that's excessive. I was literally "living" on cigarettes and Diet Dr. Pepper. In a time when I needed to be at my best, I was abusing my body and stayed physically weak and often shaky.

Another mistake I made was to trust new people in my life - particularly two men I thought were friends looking out for my best interest. I'd highly recommend that in times of crisis . . . stick to your inner circle (people with whom you have a history), and ones who have proven their character over time. Had I been in normal circumstances I would not have allowed these men to get close. As it turned out, they both added more disappointment and hurt to my already difficult situation.

I found myself working on the written response constantly . . . often through the night until 7:00 a.m. I just couldn't stop. I had extensive evidence to show that I'm telling the truth, from several different angles/sources. I felt confident that this would only be a two to three month "hiccup" in my life. God held me through each day and was literally with me through my darkest hours - in the darkness of those many nights.

I continued to serve at Lakewood and performed a drama sketch that was very intense for me . . . because I was exhausted. I still wasn't eating and I was only sleeping three to four hours a night. I looked sick without makeup and I had dark circles under my eyes. Several people came up and told me how the drama sketch touched them. Even though I wanted to withdraw from the world and hide until all this was over - I continued to be available for God to use me . . . and I was grateful to be serving at Lakewood Church.

I got to drama rehearsal early on January 16. The escalators are not operating on non-service days, but they were that night. I just got on it and went up to the second floor and right into the sanctuary. That is the first time I had ever been in the sanctuary alone . . . no one cleaning, no people passing through or praying . . . it was just me! I went to the front and the podium had been cleared so the platform was empty.

188

I walked up the stairs and stood looking out at the sanctuary. That room holds 16,000 people but it felt like a small living room . . . it was "warm." I lay down with my arms open and I prayed. I prayed for my situation and resolution, I prayed that my reputation would be restored, I prayed for rest, for peace, for wisdom . . . my mind was racing about how my life could be so upside down.

I know God is interested in every detail of our lives and I also know God gave us a brain so we will use it. There are some decisions that He has given us wisdom to make. I don't know that God really minds whether you wear the red shirt or the brown shirt, or (as Marcos Witt so eloquently said) if you eat the Snickers or the M&M's - but I do know that God has assigned Angels and Spirits to help and guide us, just as Satan has assigned Demons to destroy us. (The Bible reveals 99 references to Angels, 49 references to Spirits and 80 references to Demons.)

I've never heard God "talk" to me in an audible voice, but deep down in my Spirit, I did hear Him from the inside. He said, "Shhhhhh, Shhhhhh, Shhhhhh – I've got it . . . And I've got you - my sweet child." Tears streamed down my cheeks and I wasn't praying to Him anymore - - - I was listening to Him. His presence was all over me and I felt burning warmth throughout my body - but the room was cool and there was a slight breeze blowing over me.

I lay there in God's presence for 15-20 minutes and then knew it was time to get up and go to drama. He stirred in me that He put me in that group for a reason and there were people counting on me. Normally, I'd expect to feel a bit groggy but I felt refreshed, got up and started walking down the stairs. About half way down, I got off balance and thought I'd stood up too quickly. My body felt like I was being pressed down to sit on the stairs. I've fainted before and I know to put my head between my knees if I get dizzy, but my head wouldn't go forward. I was laid "up" the stairs and the whole room spun around. I've never experienced that before. I'd always been skeptical about people being "Slain in the Spirit." Even watching the Benny Hinn shows, I wondered what was real and what was "put on." All I know is that I presented myself - *all of me* - to God on His alter - and I experienced peace with Him that truly surpassed any understanding.

Do not be anxious about anything, but in everything, by
prayer and petition, with thanksgiving, present your requests
to God. And the peace of God, which transcends all under-

standing, will guard your hearts and your minds in Christ Jesus. Philippians 4:6-7 (NIV)

Each day I gave my anger and frustration over to God and made more of an effort to get still. I suppose you could say I was fasting noise. It was very uncomfortable and I often filled that quietness with my own thoughts. I've since learned that there were two steps I needed to take to deepen my walk with the Lord.

The first step was to empty out the awful, negative thoughts that continually raced through my mind. I had a long list of "bad guys" that had hurt me and allowed this situation to happen. I also had anger and disappointment toward high level supervisors that did not step up and stop this from happening. They will have to make account for their actions before God. Doing the right thing is not tolerating the wrong thing.

It often took quite a while to let go of all those thoughts – to empty myself of the negative - but when I did . . . I found peace.

Once I was empty and listening for God, the second step was to fill myself up with God's Word and other Christian resources (books, tapes, devotionals, etc.). I listened to a lot of Christian music (there is awesome Christian music out there no matter what style you like) and I meditated. Meditation is just reflection . . . thinking about what you just read, heard, etc. You _must_ fill yourself up with God.

> *When a defiling evil spirit is expelled from someone, it drifts along through the desert looking for an oasis, some unsuspecting soul it can bedevil. When it doesn't find anyone, it says, 'I'll go back to my old haunt.' On return it finds the person spotlessly clean, but vacant. It then runs out and rounds up seven other spirits more evil than itself and they all move in, whooping it up. That person ends up far worse off than if he'd never gotten cleaned up in the first place. That's what this generation is like: You may think you have cleaned out the junk from your lives and gotten ready for God, but you weren't hospitable to my kingdom message, and now all the devils are moving back in. Matthew 12: 43-45 (TMB)*

The passage above tells us why we (or those we love) can have a great experience with God and then things seem to get worse. It's because the person _is_ worse . . . when you see what's happening from a

Spiritual perspective. It's a problem of epidemic proportions. I hear story after story about people that go to church, have an experience with God and they're soon back to all the bad stuff. Couples can't work things out, tempers are not controlled, and destructive behaviors don't change. Why is it that people have a sincere desire to make positive changes in their lives, but they can't or won't stick with it? It even happened to Paul in the Bible:

> *So now, no longer am I the one doing it, but sin which dwells in me. For I know that nothing good dwells in me, that is, in my flesh; for the willing is present in me, but the doing of the good is not. For the good that I want, I do not do, but I practice the very evil that I do not want. But if I am doing the very thing I do not want, I am no longer the one doing it, but sin which dwells in me. Romans 7:17-20 (NASB)*

I believe there are some people that make a "show" in church for their spouse, friends or family so they are never changed by God. I even had a fiancé do that for me. But I also believe some of these people are very sincere. They do meet the Holy Spirit and are saved through Jesus Christ.

> *Therefore if anyone is in Christ, he is a new creature; the old things passed away; behold, new things have come. 2 Corinthians 5:17 (NASB)*

The problem is so often our pride. We can never work hard enough to be good . . . people can't change without God and it's often hard to let go and turn your life over. People walk away and think they can white knuckle their way to success. We need help. We need God.

> *Jesus looked at them and said, "With man this is impossible, but not with God; all things are possible with God." Mark 10:27 (NIV)*

After working so hard to forgive the people who were used for evil lies, I didn't want to be so empty that Satan just came back with more of his buddies. I filled myself up with God.

Have you ever wondered why people say, "God Bless you" when someone sneezes? There are differing opinions, one being that a sneeze forces evil out of a person and "God Bless you" is meant to protect the soul and keep the evil from re-entering. I only found two Biblical references for sneezes. The one in *Kings 4:35* is where Jesus brought Elisha's son back to life. The boy sneezed seven times and opened his eyes (defeating the evil of death) and the other is *Job 41:18* that speaks of God's power.

Although "God Bless you" to a person sneezing may be said more for cultural politeness these days, the principle of evil leaving the body and evil entering the body is based in God's Word. Think about this the next time you hear someone sneeze, or sneeze yourself. It may prompt us to pray for each other – and we all need prayer.

God was using this situation to refine me . . . to tenderize my heart for Him. I was so moved and humbled as we sang in church about God's greatness and His love. I had to embrace this difficult process and let God mold me to be what He made me to be. It reminds me of the Teacup and the Potter (Author Unknown):

> *There was a couple who used to go to England to shop in a beautiful antique store. This trip was to celebrate their 25th wedding anniversary. They both liked antiques and pottery, and especially teacups. Spotting an exceptional cup, they asked, "May we see that? We've never seen a cup quite so beautiful."*
>
> *As the lady handed it to them, suddenly the teacup spoke. "You don't understand," it said. "I haven't always been a tea-cup.*
>
> *There was a time when I was brown and I was clay. My master took me and rolled me and patted me over and over and I yelled out, 'let me alone', but he only smiled, 'Not yet.'*
>
> *Then I was placed on a spinning wheel," the teacup said, "and suddenly I was spun around and around and around. Stop it! I'm getting dizzy! I screamed. But the master only nodded and said, 'Not yet.'*

192

Then he put me in the oven. I never felt such heat. I wondered why he wanted to burn me, and I yelled and knocked at the door. I could see him through the opening and I could read his lips as he shook his head, 'Not yet.'

Finally the door opened, he put me on the shelf, and I began to cool. 'There, that's better,' I said. And he brushed and painted me all over. The fumes were horrible. I thought I would gag. 'Stop it, stop it!' I cried. He only nodded, 'Not yet.' Then suddenly he put me back into the oven, not like the first one. This was twice as hot and I knew I would suffocate. I begged. I pleaded. I screamed. I cried. All the time I could see him through the opening nodding his head saying, 'Not yet.'

Then I knew there wasn't any hope. I would never make it. I was ready to give up. But the door opened and he took me out and placed me on the shelf. One hour later he handed me a mirror and said, 'Look at yourself.' And I did. I said, 'That's not me; that couldn't be me. It's beautiful. I'm beautiful.'

'I want you to remember, then,' he said, 'I know it hurts to be rolled and patted, but if I had left you alone, you'd have dried up. I know it made you dizzy to spin around on the wheel, but if I had stopped, you would have crumbled. I knew it hurt and was hot and disagreeable in the oven, but if I hadn't put you there, you would have cracked. I know the fumes were bad when I brushed and painted you all over, but if I hadn't done that, you never would have hardened; you would not have had any color in your life. And if I hadn't put you back in that second oven, you wouldn't survive for very long because the hardness would not have held. Now you are a finished product. You are what I had in mind when I first began with you.'"

Moral: God knows what He's doing in each of us. He is the potter, and we are His clay. He will mold us and make us, and expose us to just enough pressures of just the right kinds that we may be made into a flawless piece of work to fulfill His good, pleasing and perfect will.

*When life seems hard and you are being pounded and patted
and pushed almost beyond endurance; when your world seems
to be spinning out of control; when you feel like you are in a
fiery furnace of trials; when life seems to "stink," talk to the
potter.*

*But those who wait for the Lord [who expect, look for, and
hope in Him] shall change and renew their strength and
power; they shall lift their wings and mount up [close to God]
as eagles [mount up to the sun]; they shall run and not be
weary, they shall walk and not faint or become tired.*
Isaiah 40:31 (AMP)

My family, friends and church family (Whitesburg and Lakewood)
helped me through each step of this . . . with hugs, words of encouragement and literally standing by me to lift me up. The Lakewood
Players Drama Team, led by Wendell Burton was a major source of
strength and support.

When Mr. Jeremiah and I went to the FBI office to review documents, I was bewildered that I had to interact with CDC Curt again.
Normally, an accuser would have to remove himself from further interaction with his victim. However, CDC Curt involved himself with
each and every step . . . from his false allegations to him showing me
out the door - he seemed to have personal orders to get rid of me.

I often felt like I was in the eye of a long storm. I could see things
whipping around me, but where I was standing it was calm and even
had rays of sunshine on me. There were several times throughout this
that I'd be with friends and just crack up laughing - belly laughing!!!
It was good medicine.

God was turning my sorrow into gladness and mourning into joy.
The situation wasn't changing - but God was showing me how to...

*Trust in the Lord and do good. Then you will live safely in the
land and prosper. Take delight in the Lord, and He will give
you your heart's desires. Commit everything you do to the
Lord. Trust Him, and He will help you. He will make your
innocence radiate like the dawn, and the justice of your cause
will shine like the noonday sun.*

Be still in the presence of the Lord, and wait patiently for Him to act. Don't worry about evil people who prosper or fret about their wicked schemes.

Stop being angry! Turn from your rage! Do not lose your temper— it only leads to harm. For the wicked will be destroyed, but those who trust in the Lord will possess the land. Psalm 37:3-9 (NLT)

I thought I had a pretty good relationship with God before all this happened but I began to get closer to Him, spend time with Him and get to really know Him and trust Him. A very close friend said that in years past, I spoke about God like I knew who He was . . . now I actually have a relationship with Him. I was broken when I thought that it may have taken this - a devastating blow of FBI lies to get me to the place where I'd completely and totally submit myself to God and His will for me.

Trust in the LORD with all your heart and lean not on your own understanding; in all your ways acknowledge him, and he will make your paths straight. Proverbs 3:5-6 (NIV)

As I put more and more trust in God, I started taking better care of myself. I went to the doctor and was put on prenatal vitamins to help with the crazy effects stress was having on my body, I started eating, quit smoking and started walking and playing tennis and volleyball.

I couldn't see God's resolution to my situation but I knew He had already worked out the ending. I may be shocked and devastated by what happened but none of this surprised God. He knew before I was ever born that I'd be going through this. I don't know my future and I don't know how God will work all this out for my good – but He says He will and my faith and trust are in Him.

I remember a line from the movie *The Santa Clause* where the young boy asked Tim Allen if he'd ever seen a million dollars. Tim says no and the young boy tells him, "Just because you haven't seen it doesn't mean it doesn't exist." In the same way, just because I haven't seen a resolution to my situation doesn't mean God is not working and resolving it. Faith and trust in God are very difficult when you're in the midst of a raging storm in life. But that's what faith is . . .

> *Now faith is being sure of what we hope for and certain of*
> *what we do not see. Hebrews 11:1 (NIV)*

I also experienced an illustration of this when I was asked to plan a party for Martin. I took on that challenge with four requests: 1) provide a guest list, 2) give toward the expenses, 3) provide photographs, and 4) don't ask questions.

Ester and I worked for weeks on every detail to be sure that when it was time . . . everything would be in place and be a bigger blessing to Martin than he could ever imagine. Martin went about his daily activities and couldn't see anything going on in the background . . . in fact he might have thought I was doing nothing and had completely forgotten about him. However, he trusted me to do what I said I would do. When it was the right time (the appointed time for the party – not a day before or day after) everything was in place, all the guests arrived and Martin had a great celebration.

If I could be trustworthy as a mere person, how much more is God trustworthy to do what He promises in His Word? God is my Heavenly Father . . . my Lord and Savior and He said He would take care of this situation. He also requested a few things from me: 1) love Him, 2) trust Him, 3) be faithful, and 4) don't ask questions. It took Ester and me a matter of weeks to do something wonderful for Martin. I had to ask myself how much more God, Jesus and the Holy Spirit were doing in the background to resolve my situation. I don't see them working but when it's the right time . . . I will be blessed more than I can ever imagine. The only difficulty is that I don't have the date and time. The Bible says:

> *For a thousand years in your sight are like a day that has just*
> *gone by, or like a watch in the night. Psalm 90:4 (NIV)*

I believe God appreciates a sincere heart and I reminded Him that a day for me was 24 hours and each one was difficult. I cried out to Him, "I feel like my whole life is on hold . . . my job, where I'll live, what I'll do! I need to see Your blessings in my life . . . God, resolve this! . . . And forgive me for being impatient - You have been so gracious to me . . . please forgive me for having confusion and questions when I know I just need to trust You! Help me to trust You more . . . I ask that You show me Your hand, Your way, Your will in my life."

On Wednesday, April 12, 2006, I woke up to a phone call from CDC Curt – and felt sick . . . like it was not good news. Mr. Jeremiah and I went to the office and CDC Curt (with the new ASAC) gave the news . . . the trip to Washington before the <u>FBI HQ OPR Panel</u> had no impact. They disregarded my evidence and dismissed me from the FBI. I remained professional and then went home and cried . . . and cried . . . and cried.

I had a revelation just 24 hours later. I had been so busy defending myself and trying to get back to work, that I never stopped to really see what God wanted me to do. As I looked back I understood that I should've left the FBI when I got the EEO settlement monies. There's no place for me in the FBI because I'm a woman of truth and integrity.

I knew I would continue to fight the FBI lies – but regardless of the outcome and years of court battles . . . I would never go back to being an FBI Special Agent. I felt more pride carrying a badge to work with children at Lakewood Church that I ever did carrying the FBI badge. The FBI badge didn't mean anything – it held no value because I knew of so many agents lacking integrity and lacking truth . . . carrying the same badge. It's interesting to me that it took God allowing the final dismissal for me to come to that point. I also realized that even though the FBI lies had been the most difficult thing I ever faced, I had been happier in the months since I left than I had since the FBI training at Quantico.

Dr. Elisabeth Kubler-Ross named five stages of grief people go through following a serious loss or tragedy in her book, *On Death and Dying.* I had known about them regarding the terminally ill patient or those struggling with the death of a loved one. What I didn't realize is that a serious loss could mean a divorce (death of a relationship), health (death of a lifestyle), or job (death of a career). I wanted to be "tough" and just "handle it" but as I look back I understand that I was grieving . . . and I did go through these stages.

There's no time frame for each stage and I went back and forth between them - some several times. No two people are the same. Everyone will handle loss in different ways and in their own time. Grief is painful, which makes life painful until moving to the fifth stage - Acceptance.

FIVE STAGES OF GRIEF

1) **Denial:** "This can't be happening to me."
2) **Anger:** "*Why* is this happening? Who is to blame?"
3) **Bargaining:** "Make this not happen, and in return I will
   ____."
4) **Depression:** "I'm too sad to do anything."
5) **Acceptance:** "I'm at peace with what is going to happen/has happened."

www.memorialhospital.org/library/general/stress-THE-3.html
www.helpguide.org/mental/grief_loss.htm

The original working title of this book was, *The FBI of OZ*. Everyone in the land worshiped and revered the Wizard of Oz as an all knowing, wise and powerful big fiery head that evoked fear. In actuality the Wizard was a bumbling man moving levers while hiding behind a curtain (exposed by a dog). The FBI is much the same . . . the FBI Director is that bumbling man, supervisors are the Wicked Witches, SWAT and special teams are the flying monkeys and the street agents reside in Munchkin Land. That would make me Dorothy in this scenario and I even have a little dog.

It would make for an entertaining story but the truth is that God was with me through my darkest hours as an FBI SA and He has a much bigger plan for my life. As you'll recall from the Introduction to this book, my earthly father would not tolerate me (a daughter he loves) being involved with a group where lies were told . . . and tolerated. I did nothing wrong but my father removed me from the situation. He also rewarded me with a First Place trophy.

In this situation, I believe my Heavenly Father is doing the same thing. I am His daughter and He loves me. He would not tolerate me being a part of the FBI – where lies are told . . . and tolerated. Though

I did nothing wrong, God allowed the situation so He could remove me from that organization. I believe God will also reward me with His First Place trophy.

ௐௐௐௐௐௐ

In this you greatly rejoice, though now for a little while you may have had to suffer grief in all kinds of trials. These have come so that your faith—of greater worth than gold, which perishes even though refined by fire— may be proved genuine and may result in praise, glory and honor when Jesus Christ is revealed.
1 Peter 1:6-7 (NIV)

❧ *13* ❧

Your FBI

For the LORD watches over the way of the righteous, but the way of the wicked will perish. Psalm 1:6 (NIV)

❧❧❧❧❧❧❧

You've read my story and know many of my struggles, disappointments, suffering and trials. I know I'm not alone in suffering . . . life is full of it. I found a lot of pain in the FBI but pain comes in many shapes and sizes. Pain may come from death, divorce, an unhealthy relationship, a deep physical or emotional wound, loneliness, a rebellious child, a careless friend, financial struggle, a past or present abuse, random violence, etc. Each and every person on this earth will face their own pain . . . their own FBI – **F**aith **B**uilding **I**ncident.

Whatever your situation, I pray that you will know God is the only answer. He is Bigger than your FBI – Bigger than problems, jobs or relationships – Bigger than anything you will ever face. He loved you enough to send His only son; a perfect, sinless man, and allow Him to be beaten and crucified (as the blood sacrifice for your sins), so you can be forgiven and live for eternity with God. He loves you more than you could ever think or imagine. But you have to take the step to accept Jesus into your heart - and trust God in every situation, even when you don't understand it.

> *Delight yourself in the LORD and He will give you the desires of your heart. Psalm 37:4 (NIV)*

I've heard many an intelligent person say that God knows what a "good" person they are and God will always be there for them. The truth is that you can never be good apart from Jesus Christ and without accepting Jesus as your Lord and Savior – you will never be with God. The following scriptures explain God's truth through His Word . . .

~ *YOU ARE A SINNER* ~
For all have sinned and fall short of the glory of God.
Romans 3:23 (NIV)

~ *SINNERS DESERVE DEATH* ~
For the wages of sin is death, but the free gift of God is eternal life through Christ Jesus our Lord. Romans 6:23 (NLT)

~ *YOU CAN'T BE "GOOD" AND*
WORK YOUR WAY INTO HEAVEN ~
For it is by grace you have been saved, through faith - and this not from yourselves, it is the gift of God.
Ephesians 2:8 (NIV)

~ *GOD LOVES YOU AND GAVE HIS SON*
AS PAYMENT FOR YOUR SIN ~
For God so loved the world that he gave his only begotten Son, that whoever believes in Him shall not perish but have eternal life. John 3:16 (NIV)

~ *JESUS IS THE ONLY WAY TO GOD . . .*
TO BE SAVED FROM ETERNAL DEATH ~
Jesus answered, "I am the way and the truth and the life. No one comes to the Father except through me. John 14:6 (NIV)

Jesus answered him, I assure you, most solemnly I tell you, that unless a person is born again (anew, from above), he cannot ever see (know, be acquainted with, and experience) the kingdom of God. John 3:3 (AMP)

DON'T WAIT...
NOW IS THE TIME TO
~ ACCEPT JESUS AS YOUR LORD & SAVIOR ~

For God says, "At just the right time, I heard you. On the day of salvation, I helped you." Indeed, the "right time" is now. Today is the day of salvation. 2 Corinthians 6:2 (NLT)

That if you confess with your mouth, "Jesus is Lord," and believe in your heart that God raised him from the dead, you will be saved. Romans 10:9 (NIV)

You can accept Jesus as your Savior right now. Just pray with a sincere heart - and audibly *"confess with your mouth"*. . .

Heavenly Father God, I know that I have sinned against You. Please forgive me. I believe Jesus is Your only Son, that He lived on this earth as a perfect sinless man and was beaten and crucified as payment for my sin. I believe Jesus was buried and overcame death and hell to rise and be with You in heaven. God, I ask that You come into my heart - wash me in the cleaning blood of Your Son. Jesus is now my Lord and Savior. God, thank You for loving me and saving me by Your grace. Please fill me with Your Holy Spirit and help me to serve You with my whole heart every day of my life. In Jesus' name I pray, Amen.

∞∞∞∞∞∞∞

If you prayed that for the first time . . .
Welcome to the family of God!

∞∞∞∞∞∞∞

Satan is not happy about your decision and he will make things difficult for you in the days ahead. Many people have asked why their lives seemed to be going great until they surrendered to the Lord. When you understand how evil and wicked Satan is . . . you'll begin to understand how he works.

202

For those that do not accept Jesus, this earth is the best they will ever know. After they die, they will spend eternity in hell – exactly what Satan wants. Many times Satan gives them things on earth so they'll never have a "need" for God . . . maybe a great job, a spouse, children, friends – they seem to "have it all" – and Satan keeps them "satisfied."

However, when those people realize they are empty and no amount of "stuff" can save them – they come to Jesus and all hell breaks loose - literally. Satan does not want you to be effective for God. If he can get you angry, discouraged or depressed, you cannot live the victorious life God has for you. I often remember the following verses as the cornerstone to my Christian walk:

> *The LORD is my strength and my shield; my heart trusts in Him, and I am helped. My heart leaps for joy and I will give thanks to him in song. Psalm 28:7 (NIV)*

And *Nehemiah 8:10...*
This day is holy to our Lord. And be not grieved and depressed, for the joy of the Lord is your strength and stronghold.

Joy is not simply being "happy" – it's a peace and well-being that reaches to your soul. Clearly, if Satan can get your focus off God and take away your joy in being with God, he can get you down and depressed. Without God's joy you won't have His strength, nor live the great life God planned for you.

God is much more interested in your character than your circumstances and He will allow things in your life that will lead you to a deeper relationship with Him and refine you into the amazing creation He made you to be. Change and growth can be difficult but God has a purpose for what you experience – regardless of whether you perceive it as good or bad . . . and He will be with you every step of the way.

Do not be anxious about anything, but in everything, by prayer and petition, with thanksgiving, present your requests to God. And the peace of God, which transcends all understanding, will guard your hearts and your minds in Christ Jesus. Philippians 4:6-7 (NIV)

In our earthly relationships we have to spend time with someone to know them. The same is true with God. Spend time with Him . . . pray, read His Word – the Bible (His personal letters to you) and learn about Him by going to a Bible-teaching church, spend time with other Christians, listen to Christian music (Chris Tomlin is amazing) and read encouraging and inspirational books (Joel Osteen - *Become a Better You*). If you're not familiar with Christian authors, you might start with Beth Moore, Max Lucado and Joyce Meyer.

There's a lot of information out there and that's why it's important to know the truth of the Bible. Make sure what you read lines up with God's Word - otherwise you're not reading truth.

I pray that this book has given you insight and encouraged you to always see that…

God Is Bigger Than Your FBI

∼∼∼∼∼∼∼

May God richly bless you and give you His peace!

∼∼∼∼∼∼∼

www.TracyBaldwin.com

The Lord is My Real Boss
(Source Unknown)

The Lord is my real Boss, and I shall not want.
He gives me peace when chaos is all around me.
He gently reminds me to pray before I speak
and to do all things without murmuring or complaining.
He reminds me that He is my Source and not my job.
He restores my sanity every day and
guides my decisions that I might honor Him in everything I do.
Even though I face absurd amounts of emails,
system crashes, unrealistic deadlines, budget cutbacks,
gossiping coworkers, discriminating supervisors,
and an aging body that doesn't cooperate every morning,
I will not stop – for He is with me!
His presence, His peace, and His power
will see me through.
He raises me up, even when they fail to promote me.
He claims me as His own.
Even when the company threatens to let me go,
His faithfulness and love are better than any bonus check.
His retirement plan beats every 401K there is!
When it's all said and done,
I'll be working for Him a whole lot longer
and for that, I bless His Name.

Amen

❧❧❧❧❧❧

You have loved righteousness and hated wickedness;
therefore God, your God, has set you above your com-
panions by anointing you with the oil of joy.
Hebrews 1:9 (NIV)

Acronym List - 1
܂܂܂܂܂܂

A/	-	Acting position due to a vacancy
ANSIR	-	Awareness of National Security Issues & Response
ASAC	-	Assistant Special Agent in Charge (# 2 in charge of each FBI field office)
ASK	-	American School of Kuwait
AUO	-	Administratively Uncontrollable Overtime
AUSA	-	Assistant United States Attorney
BAU	-	Behavior Analysis Unit
BIA	-	Bureau of Indian Affairs
BMDS	-	Ballistic Missile Defense Systems
BS	-	Bluff-n-Stuff
CC	-	Command Center
CDC	-	Chief Division Counsel
CFC	-	Combined Federal Campaign
DEA	-	Drug Enforcement Administration
DOJ	-	Department of Justice
DT	-	Defensive Tactics
EAP	-	Employee Assistance Program
EEO	-	Equal Employment Opportunity
ERT	-	Evidence Response Team
ET	-	Electronics Technician
FBI	-	Federal Bureau of Investigation
FCI	-	Foreign Counter-Intelligence
FOIPA	-	Freedom Of Information Privacy Act
GETA	-	Government Employment Training Association
HQ	-	Headquarters
ICE	-	Immigration and Customs Enforcement
IPC	-	Intern Program Coordinator
KISS	-	Keep It Simple Stupid
MAOP	-	Manual of Administrative Operations & Procedures
NA	-	National Academy
NAC	-	New Agent Class
NIPC	-	National Infrastructure Protection Center

Acronym List - 2
ია ია ია ია ია

OCD	-	Obsessive Compulsive Disorder
OPR	-	Office of Professional Responsibility (FBI Internal Affairs)
PAU	-	Practical Applications Unit
PT	-	Physical Training
RS	-	Relief Supervisor
S/AUSA	-	Supervisory Assistant United States Attorney
SA	-	Special Agent
SAC	-	Special Agent in Charge (# 1 in charge of each FBI field office)
SOM	-	Special Operations Module
SSA	-	Supervisory Special Agent
SSG	-	Special Surveillance Group
SWAT	-	Special Weapons and Tactics
TA	-	Training Agent
TDY	-	Temporary Duty
TEVOC	-	Tactical Emergency Vehicle Operations Center
TMI	-	Too Much Information
UCA	-	Under Cover Agent
US	-	United States
WCC	-	White Collar Crime
WHL	-	Wen Ho Lee
WWW	-	World Wide Web
Y2K	-	Year 2000
*****	-	Inappropriate Language

Website References
✍✍✍✍✍✍

"Bright Line" Policy: www.usdoj.gov/oig/special/0211/chapter6.htm

BADGE: www.findarticles.com/p/articles/mi_m1355/is_23_99/ai_75021588

Big John Shropshire: www.r-sports.com /hsf/Aerobics/johnshro.htm

Dippin' Dots: www.dippindots.com

EEO Government Protection: eeoc.gov/types/retaliation.html

EEO Info, Where's My Parade! Tracy L. Baldwin: www.eeoinfo.com

FBI Academy Training: www.fbi.gov/hq/td/academy/sat/sat.htm

FBI Applicant Requirements: www.fbijobs.gov

FBI Core Values: www.fbi.gov/priorities/priorities.htm

FBI HQ Structure: www.fbi.gov/page2/july06/orgchart072606.pdf

FBI SA Miami Firefight: www.foia.fbi.gov/foiaindex/shooting.htm

FBI Seal: www.fbi.gov/libref/historic/fbiseal/fbiseal.htm

FBI Seeks Women Special Agents article: www.fbijobs.gov/041.asp

FBI Whistleblowers: www.fbiwhistlestop.com

Grief: www.memorialhospital.org/library/general/stress-THE-3.html
www.helpguide.org/mental/grief_loss.htm

Healthy Soul Seminar - Leo Tyler: www.HealthySoul.org

Hoover: www.crimelibrary.com/gangsters_outlaws/cops_others/hoover/6.html

Merriam-Webster Online: www.m-w.com

OPR Bell/Colwell Report: www.fbi.gov/publications/opr/bellreport.pdf

Patriot Act: www.cbsnews.com/stories/2007/03/27/terror/main2613379.shtml

SA Ahrens Killed: www.fbi.gov/libref/hallhonor/ahrens.htm

The Holy Grail script: www.angelfire.com/ny5/mpholygrail/script.html

VA Tech Shoot: www.cnn.com/2007/US/04/17/vtech.shooting/index.html

www.TracyBaldwin.com